Become
an
EFFECTIVE
Leader

Become an EFFECTIVE Leader

DALE CARNEGIE

MANJUL

Manjul Publishing House

First published in India by

MANJUL

Manjul Publishing House

● C-16, Sector 3, Noida, Uttar Pradesh 201301, India
Website: www.manjulindia.com
Registered Office:
●2nd Floor, Usha Preet Complex, 42 Malviya Nagar, Bhopal 462 003 - India

Distribution Centres
Ahmedabad, Bengaluru, Kochi, Kolkata, Chennai,
Hyderabad, Mumbai, New Delhi, Pune
The Success Series:
Become an Effective Leader by *Dale Carnegie*

This edition first published in India in 2018
Fourth impression 2025

Copyright © Dale Carnegie & Associates
Rights licensed exclusively by JMW Group Inc.
jmwgroup@jmwgroup.net

ISBN   978-93-87383-31-9

Cover Design by Trinankur Banerjee

This edition is authorised for sale in the Indian Subcontinant only.

Printed and bound in India by Repro India Ltd.

CONTENTS

PREFACE

Are successful managers more concerned with meeting established goals or leading the people they supervise? Effective managers know that in order to reach those goals, they must be true leaders, who guide, motivate, coach, and care for their associates. Balancing the skills between leadership and management should be the focus of all who aspire to succeed in their jobs.

It is important to examine the balance between what we are doing versus what we are leading others to do. How can we identify and leverage our leadership style to be the best we can be in order to get the best results for ourselves and our organization?

The way we see others and the assumptions we make about people and the world around us shape our reality and the environment in which we work. In this book we examine the lessons we have learned about leadership and the beliefs we form as a result of those experiences.

The Changing Role of the Manager/Leader

The world is rapidly changing and requires those in leadership and management positions to assume constantly changing roles and responsibilities. Whether we are in Europe, Africa, the Americas, or the Pacific Rim, competition constantly demands that we find better, more efficient, more productive, and more profitable ways to produce products and deliver services.

These demands are not limited to our competition— The expectations of our people, our internal and external customers, our suppliers, distributors, and business partners are increasing. In order for us to remain competitive in today's rapidly changing world, we lead and manage our organizations through the 21st century.

Create and Share a Vision

We must be creative and create a shared vision, and communicate effectively with our associates. We must encourage our people to step outside the box created by job descriptions and a minimalistic approach to the work world so that our companies will grow and prosper in today's world. It is critical that we hire and cultivate people who are capable of helping us move our organizations to the next level. We cannot do this ourselves nor can our people help us move to the next level, unless we first identify our goals and establish and communicate a clear vision to our associates. Once a shared vision is created and disseminated throughout the organization, the resultant empowered behavior catapults us to the next level. People cease viewing their role as task-oriented and instead become results-oriented. Clearly seeing outcomes inspires one and one's associates to take risks and responsibility. Leadership begins finding its own level in the organization. Clearly focused outcomes allow people to become more self-managed and to handle resources without senior level assistance.

Empowered behavior is driven by a shared vision, but neither is possible unless the vision is clearly communicated throughout the organization. Effective communication is the foundational skill of building effective teams, creating a unified sense of purpose, and moving our organization to the next level.

Balancing People and Process

When asked to identify the most significant personal characteristic needed by management, most senior executives say, "the ability to work with people." Leaders recognize the importance of production, distribution, engineering, sales, research and development, and they have management systems in place to organize, direct, and control activities in each area. However, when it is time to carry out executive decisions, they are carried out by people. The largest single operating expense in any budget is people. Planning, whether functional or strategic, is carried out and built around people. The most valuable asset an organization has is its people. In fact, most executives spend approximately three-fourths of every working day dealing with people. This means that we create the management system by which our organization functions and continually demonstrate leadership that allows those systems to achieve their objectives.

One of the main reasons people are promoted into management and leadership positions is because they were effective at what they did in their job. Now, as a manager, the job is to get others to be able to do things as well as or better than we did them. These require a totally different skill set. Our success requires making the transition from doing to leading in order to leverage our skills and our time.

To be effective as a manager we must balance people and process. Being too people focused mean that if a key person leaves, everything stops. Being too process focused means that great systems are in place; however no one understands them or wants to work within them. Process focus says: "Here's the plan and here's how we do things." People focus says: "Let's discuss the plan and why we do things." With the right balance, both productivity and commitment stay at their highest levels.

Balancing Motivation and Accountability

Without motivation nothing gets done but as soon as we try to hold people accountable they get demotivated, right? Not necessarily! There are tools to hold people accountable for their goals, objectives, and commitments, and stay motivated at the same time. With this balance, we have more control over results for ourselves and our team.

Today, more than ever, a manager's job is to build people. When we can create an environment where people get results, develop new skills, and become successful, we are fulfilling our highest calling as a manager and leader of people. Communicating with strength and sensitivity, being a coach, and building people are a leader's highest priority.

Handling Conflict and Negativity

No matter what we do there will always be the challenges with negative people and performance management. Our results, and the results of our team, depend on how those situations are handled. Fairness, consistency, and strength are required in the right places, at the right times and in the right way. Without this, morale can grind to a halt for everyone, effecting productivity, customer loyalty, and employee loyalty—all mandatory in today's highly competitive work force.

In this book we will tackle these and other problems leaders face and provide approaches that will enable us and our associates to improve productivity and at the same time develop skills, attitudes, and capabilities that will help all of us grow in our jobs.

To get the most out of this book, read all of it first to absorb the overall concept of dealing with our roles as leaders. Then reread each chapter and start applying the guidelines for achieving each of the areas covered.

Arthur R. Pell, Ph.D.
Editor

1

....

DON'T BOSS—LEAD

Peter Drucker, one of the greatest management thinkers, wrote: "Most of what we call management consists of making it difficult for people to get their work done."

What is it that managers do that instigated Drucker to write that? Many people in managerial or supervisory positions deal with their people as if they were automatons—expecting them to follow procedures exactly and not use any of their own initiative, creativity, and brain power when working. They are so concerned with following rules, regulations, procedures, and routines that they overlook the potential that each human being working under their supervision may have.

Managers, who truly lead their people instead of directing their work, not only obtain better results for their organizations, but develop teams of people who are committed to working toward success in every aspect of their jobs and their lives.

Do you know the most important trait a leader can have? It is not executive ability; it is not a great mentality; it is not kindliness, nor courage, not a sense of humor, though each of those is of tremendous importance. It is the ability to make friends, which boiled down, means the ability to see the best in others.

Dale Carnegie

Leaders Serve

The true leader serves his or her people, not the other way around. The typical geometric figure we associate with most organizations is the triangle. On the top is the boss who gives orders to middle management who gives orders to supervisors who in turn give orders to the workers. At the very bottom of the triangle are the customers who we hope will be satisfied by what we provide.

The purpose of each layer is to serve the layer above it. In the traditional approach, workers serve their supervisors, supervisors, their managers, and all eventually serve the big boss. The customer, down at the bottom is virtually ignored. The triangle should be reversed. Top level management should serve the middle level managers, who in turn serve their first line supervisors, who are there to serve the workers—and all serve the customer.

Leaders Serve their Staffs

J. Willard Marriott, the hotel entrepreneur, sums it up succinctly: "My job is to motivate my people, teach them, help them and care about them." Note that last item—care about them. Good leaders truly care about their people. They learn as much as they can about their strengths and limitations, their likes and their dislikes, how they act and react. They take the time to work with them, to give them the resources, the tools, the know-how to do their job effectively. They do not get in their way by worrying more about whether every "i" is dotted and every "t" crossed.

When surveys are made on what people want from a boss, almost the very top item is a *boss who is there for me.* This is a boss to whom a person can come with a question and not be afraid of being thought to be stupid; a boss on whom one can depend to provide information, training, and suggestions rather than make demands, and give orders and commands. This is a boss who helps develop the potential of people—not just use them merely as a means of getting a job done.

Empower Our People

Real leaders "empower" their people. This word *empower* has become a fad word in management today, but fad words often express concisely a currently accepted concept. It derives from a legal term meaning transferring certain legal rights from one person to another. In today's management parlance, however, it is used in a broader sense—to share some of the authority and control a manager has with the people who he or she manages. Instead of the manager making every decision as to how a job should be done, the people who perform the job participate in doing this. When people have some say in these determinations, not only will we obtain more varied information as to how a job can be done, but because they did participate, the workers become committed to its success.

Managing versus Leading

Managing emphasizes that people follow orders—often unquestioningly. "This is the way it's going to be done." Leading encourages creativity in people by soliciting their ideas both informally in day to day contact and formally in meetings, suggestion programs and similar activities. Managing is telling people what they will be accountable for. Leading empowers people—giving them the tools to make their own decisions within guidelines that are acceptable to all parties concerned.

Managing is more concerned with how the policies are followed, explaining rules and policies, and enforcing them. Leading motivates people and teaches them how to get the job done. If it doesn't work out as expected, efforts are made to improve performance by better training. Helping people learn is the key tool in obtaining quality performance.

Managing concentrates efforts on *doing things right;* leading emphasize *doing the right things.* There are times when it is necessary to manage—when for legal or similar reasons, it is essential that things be done according to the book. Of course, people in managerial positions must assure that things are done right, but this is not their main job. Enforcing rules may be necessary in such circumstances, but more important is to train and motivate people to be competent and desirous of doing their very best to meet the department and the company's objectives. To achieve this with one's people is the epitome of true leadership.

Good Boss—Bad Boss

Harry was the kind of boss that liked to be popular. He thought he was a good boss because everybody in his department liked him. He did not want to upset this popularity so he hesitated to enforce minor infractions of rules or correct minor errors in work. When a reprimand was called for, he would stall it for so long that the reason for it was often forgotten. However, praise was so common that it lost significance.

Teresa was tough. She believed that one had to crack the whip to get the work done. She was abrupt, dogmatic and her favorite expression was: "I am the boss. You get paid to work so you'd better work or else." She rarely praised her people and often bawled them out in front of the whole department.

Both Harry and Teresa had serious problems because neither of these extremes could really work. Let's look at what happened in each of these areas.

The Easy-Going Boss

When a manager does not control the department, the work will be affected. Production schedules will not be met, quality suffers, people take advantage of this leniency and absenteeism, tardiness, and general attitudes deteriorate. Harry's people feel leaderless and walk all over him.

Why will a manager become so lenient and easy-going to the point where the department suffers? Often it can be traced to a feeling of insecurity in one's own ability. Insecure persons demand approval from others to bolster one's own ego. Such people want to be popular, to be "one of the gang." They believe that leniency with subordinates will engender employee approval.

When Harry's boss discovers that the department is falling behind, Harry will be held accountable. Now, Harry gets nervous as it is clear that he has to reverse this rapidly. A natural reaction is to do an abrupt about-face. He begins to get tough and demanding. He jumps on his people, often hollering, and screaming. He begins to reprimand people for every minor violation and punish people for matters he had ignored only a week earlier. This causes resentment and uncertainty among his people. The work may pick up for a while, but as the nature of Harry's personality is quite the opposite of these actions, once things straighten out, he reverts to his old self.

Frequent changes in management style are more demoralizing than sticking to one style—good or bad. Our people cannot anticipate how we will behave. This uncertainty leads to poor morale and heavy turnover.

The cause of Harry's easy-going attitude stems from his own sense of insecurity. He has to build up his self-confidence—One way of accomplishing this is to become expert in the work one does. When a person is thoroughly knowledgeable about the work, there is a feeling of security in it that leads to self-confidence in all matters pertaining to the work. He should also study more about human relations and apply what he has learned to his job.

The Hard-Boiled Supervisor

Teresa has a similar problem. Although her style is quite different from Harry's, the results are much the same. She causes resentment among her people—consciously or subconsciously, they refuse to cooperate. Lower production, higher turnover, more absenteeism, numerous grievances, and generally poor morale are the usual evidences of such a lack of cooperation.

The cause of the tough approach as of the lenient one is insecurity. However, the "desire to please" attitude is replaced by a gruff manner and authoritarian veneer. It is more difficult for hard-boiled leaders to change, probably because they have a stubborn feeling that their way is the only way. Stubbornness is an integral part of their behavior pattern.

Again the solution requires a good knowledge of human relations. The supervisor must learn to praise more frequently, and how to administer effective reprimands without causing resentment and rancor. Teresa must learn to tone down her manner and speech to avoid arguments and to work more amiably with her co-workers and staff.

The Best Supervisor

The most effective supervisory style is somewhere between these two extremes. It is grounded on understanding human behavior and applying this knowledge in working with the people under his or her jurisdiction. He or she praises people for good work, but does not throw praise around lightly. Harry overdid praise to the point that none of his people felt that their remarkably good work was really appreciated. Teresa never praised her people so they felt that there was no point in doing remarkably good work.

Reprimanding, where called for, should be done in private and in a calm manner. Never raise one's voice and always give the employee the opportunity to tell his or her own side of the story. Listen attentively and do not interrupt. Give constructive criticism and be as specific as possible.

Do not reprimand in a bad mood or in anger. Do not get maneuvered into an argument. Avoid sarcasm and nagging.

Keep to the issues. Remember the purpose of a reprimand is to right a wrong. A good manager would not want to compound the wrong by creating resentment. Always emphasize the *what* rather than the *who*. Suggestions on how to give effective reprimands will be discussed in chapter 9.

Good leaders are neither wishy-washy hail-fellow-well-met characters nor tyrants. They are neither ignored nor feared by their subordinates. Capable supervisors have inner confidence plus the respect of their people.

Let's look at a simple comparison between the way a boss manages and a leader leads:

The Boss as The Leader

Instills Fear
Says 'Do'
Makes work drudgery
Relies upon authority
Says 'I', 'I', 'I'

Myths and Misconceptions

Myths and misconceptions that have governed people's thinking for years or for lifetimes are tough to overcome. As a manager, however, we must shatter them if we want to be able to move ahead.

Some people are reluctant to take on leadership roles. To do so, they believe that they would have to have certain innate leadership traits such as charisma, or that intangible personality that would empower them to influence others.

It's true that some of the world's greatest leaders were born that way—they had that special charm that enraptured the public. But they are the exceptions. The majority of successful leaders are ordinary men and women who have worked hard to get where they are. Management of people is easier if we have natural talents, but they're not essential. Each of us can certainly acquire the skills necessary to manage and lead people.

Leadership is an art that can be acquired. With a little effort anybody who desires to can learn to guide people in a way that commands their respect, confidence, and whole-hearted cooperation.

Many managers like to refer to themselves as "professionals," but is management really a profession? Professionals in other fields (such as physicians, lawyers, psychologists, and engineers) are required to complete advanced study and pass exams for certification. There are no such requirements to be a manager. Some managers may have special education such as degrees in business administration, but most are promoted from the ranks and have little or no training in management. Most managers learn primarily on the job.

More and more successful managers are making an effort to acquire skills through structured courses of study, but most managers still pick up their techniques by observing their bosses. The model they follow may be good. Too often, however, new managers are exposed to their bosses' outdated and invalid philosophies.

Some of these ideas noted below may have been valid in the past but are no longer effective; others were never true. Let's look at some of the many myths and misconceptions about management.

Management is No More than Common Sense

A manager was asked about his training when he started in management, he said, "When I was promoted to my first management job, I asked a long-time manager for some tips about how to deal with people who report to me. He told me, 'Just use common sense and you'll have no trouble.'"

What is "common sense," exactly? What appears to be sensible to one person may be nonsense to another. Often the definition of "common sense" is culturally based. In Japan, for example, it's considered "common sense" to wait for a full consensus before making any decision; in the United States, this technique is often derided as inefficient and a waste of time.

Cultural customs aren't the only cause for differing ideas about what constitutes common sense. Different people have different views about what is good and what is bad, what is efficient and what is wasteful, and what will work and what will not.

We tend to use our own experiences to develop our particular brands of common sense. The problem is, a person's individual experience provides only limited perspective. Although what we think of as common sense has been developed from our own experiences; an individual's experience is never enough to provide anything other than limited perspectives. Leadership involves much more than the experience an individual may have. To be a real leader, we must look beyond common sense.

We wouldn't rely solely on common sense to help with financial or manufacturing problems. We would call on the best possible expertise in these areas for advice and information.

Why then should we resort to a less pragmatic base in handling human-relations problems?

We can learn a lot about the art and science of management by reading industry-related books and periodicals in the field, attending courses and seminars, and actively participating in industry associations.

Managers Know Everything

Managers don't know everything. Nobody does. Accept that we don't have all the answers, but know that we need the skills to get the answers. One effective way is to develop contacts with people in other companies who have faced similar situations. We can learn a great deal from them. Networking—making contacts with people in other companies to whom we can turn for suggestions, ideas, and problem-solving strategies—gives us access to these people when we need new information and ideas, and provides us with a valuable ongoing resource for assistance in solving problems.

> *Don't you have much more fate in ideas that you discover yourself than ideas that are handed down to you? If so, isn't it bad judgment to ram your ideas down the throats of other people? Wouldn't it be wise to make suggestions and let the other person think out the conclusion for themselves?*

Dale Carnegie

It's My Way or the Highway!

Management using fear is still a common practice. And it

works, sometimes. People will work if they fear that they might lose their jobs, but how much work will they do? The answer is "Just enough to keep from getting fired." That's why this technique isn't considered effective management. Successful management involves getting the willing cooperation of our associates.

Moreover, it's not that easy to fire people. Considering the implications of the civil-rights laws and labor unions—and in many cases the difficulty and costs associated with hiring competent replacements—firing people may cause more problems than keeping employees with whom we are not satisfied.

We can't keep good workers for long when we manage by fear. When jobs are scarce in our community or industry, workers might tolerate high-handed, arbitrary bosses, but when the job market opens up, the best people will leave for companies with more pleasant working environments. Employee turnover can be expensive and often devastating.

Praising Is Coddling Employees

Some managers fear that if they praise a team member's work, that person will become complacent and stop trying to improve (certainly, some people do react this way). The objective key is to phrase our praise in a manner that encourages the associate to keep up the good work.

Other managers are concerned that if associates are praised for good work, they will expect pay raises or bonuses. And some folks might. But that's no reason to withhold praise when it's warranted. Employees should know how salary adjustments, bonuses, and other financial rewards are determined. If compensation is renegotiated at annual performance evaluations, team members should be assured that the good work for which they are praised will be considered in the evaluation.

Some managers consider praise irrelevant. One department head reported, "The people I supervise know that they're doing okay if I don't talk to them. If I have to speak to them, they know they are in trouble." Offering no feedback other than reprimands, isn't effective either. Remember, we want to use positive, not negative, reinforcement.

Of course, praise can be overdone. If people are repeatedly praised for every trivial accomplishment, the value of praise is diminished to the point of being becoming superficial. Also, nonproductive employees can think they're doing great if they are praised excessively. Techniques on effective use of praise will be discussed in chapter 3.

Let's praise the slightest improvement that inspires the other person to keep on improving.

Dale Carnegie

Using the Whip Excessively

Sure, some managers still act as slave masters. Every year James Miller, management consultant and the author of 'The Corporate Coach,' holds a contest for the Best and Worst Boss of the Year. Employees do the nominating. Miller reports that he gets many more nominations for worst boss than for best boss. One of the chief reasons employees dislike their bosses, Miller found, is that these bosses are continually finding fault with subordinates, expressing sarcasm, gloating over failures, and frequently hollering and screaming at employees.

Why do people behave this way? Some people have always been screamed at—by parents, teachers, and former bosses—so they may assume that it's an effective communication tool.

We all raise our voices occasionally, especially when we're under stress. Sometimes it takes great self-discipline not to yell. Effective leaders, however, control this tendency. An occasional lapse is okay, but when yelling becomes our normal manner of communication, we're admitting our failure to be real leaders. We cannot get the willing cooperation of our associates by screaming at them.

Try the Platinum Rule

When we manage people, the Biblical golden rule, "Do unto others as you would have others do unto you" is sound advice, but only to a point. People are not all alike; treating others as we want to be treated is not the same as treating them as they want to be treated.

For example, Linda prefers to be given broad objectives and likes to work out the details of her job on her own. But her assistant, Jason, is not comfortable receiving an assignment unless all the details are spelled out for him. If Linda delegates work to her assistant in the way she likes to have work assigned to her, she won't get the best results.

Sol needs continuous reinforcement. He's happy on the job only when his boss oversees his work and assures Sol that he's doing a good job. Tanya, however, gets upset if her boss checks her work too often. "Doesn't she trust me?" she complains. We can't do unto Tanya as we do unto Sol and get good results from each of them.

Each of us has our own style, our own approach, and

our own eccentricities. To "do unto others" as we would have them do unto us may be the poorest way of managing people.

To be an effective manager, we must know each member of our team and tailor our method of management to each person's individuality. Rather than follow the golden rule, follow the platinum rule: *Do unto others as they would have you do unto them.*

Compromises must be made, of course. In some situations, work must be done in a manner that may not be ideal for some people. By knowing ahead of time what needs to be accomplished, we can anticipate problems and prepare our associates to accept their tasks.

Leaders Must Produce More than Optimum Performance

Production, performance, and profit are important aspects of our job as managers, but are these all we have to consider? Certainly, if a business is to survive, it must produce results. Equally important, however, is the development of its employees. If we ignore people's potential, our team's ability to attain results is limited. Instead, we reap short-term benefits at the expense of long-term success and even survival.

When Eliot founded his computer-components company, he was a pioneer in what was then a new and growing industry. Determined to be a leader in his field, he drove his employees to maintain high levels of productivity, and kept his eye carefully trained on the profit picture. But he paid no attention to the development of his staff. His technical and administrative staff members were given little opportunity to contribute ideas or use their own initiative on their own projects. Over the years, Eliot's company saw reasonable profits, but it never grew to become an industry-leader as he had hoped. Because he had stifled the potential and ambition of his employees, he lost many of his technical staff members to other companies. And because he depended only on his own ideas, he missed out on all the innovative ideas his staff might have come up with.

Sum and Substance

> Leadership is an art that can be acquired. With a little effort anybody who desires to can learn to guide people in a way that commands their respect, confidence, and whole-hearted cooperation.
> Don't boss—lead.
> Managers are often influenced by misconceptions and myths about management. Don't automatically follow in an old boss's footsteps.
> Be neither hard-boiled nor easy-going. The most effective supervisory style is somewhere between these two extremes. It is grounded on understanding human behaviour and applying this knowledge in working with the people under his or her jurisdiction.
> Praise people for work done well. Unrecognized work is like an un-watered plant. Productivity will wither away.
> Follow the platinum rule: "Do Unto Others as they would have you do unto them."
> We must always be there for our people.

2

....

CHARACTERISTICS OF
SUCCESSFUL LEADERS

One need not be born a leader; most people can be trained to be leaders, but there are characteristics that they must acquire to be truly great leaders. Over the years many studies have been made on what these characteristics are.

Although individual strengths and abilities may vary, research indicates that outstanding managers view the world in similar ways. The following represent the most commonly observed qualities of successful leaders:

1. *They hold strong values and high ethical standards.* We can learn a lot by following the philosophy of Sir John Templeton, the founder of the Templeton Fund, one of the world's most profitable mutual funds. He bases his business practices on the belief that the most successful people are often the most ethically motivated.

He says that such people are likely to have the keenest understanding of the importance of morality in business, and can be trusted to give full measure and not cheat their customers.

Hard work combined with honesty and perseverance is the crux of the Templeton philosophy. "Individuals who have learned to invest themselves in their work are successful. They have earned what they have. More than simply knowing the value of money, they know their own value."

2. *They lead by example, acting with integrity in both their professional and personal lives.* Whether it is carrying out their own ideas or those of others, they work to assure that what has been planned is achieved. Nothing is more powerful in reinforcing leadership skills than success and achievements. Working hard to accomplish the goals set by the leader and his or her associates will enhance the probability of success and motivate the leader and the group to move ahead.

3. *They are knowledgeable about corporate and department goals and stay informed of changes.* The best leaders set high standards for themselves and then work hard to achieve their goals. Like everyone, we will make mistakes; and when we do, we must view these mistakes as learning experiences and try to turn them into successes. As it has been said: "If you've never made errors, you've never made decisions."

4. *They are proactive and self-motivated to achieve results.* They are never entirely satisfied with themselves. They keep up not only with the state of the art in their fields, but they improve their knowledge and understanding in a variety of areas. They read professional journals and magazines in their

areas of interest. They read extensively. They take active roles in professional and trade associations not only to keep in touch with new developments, but to share their ideas with colleagues from other organizations. They attend and participate in conventions and conferences and develop networks of people to whom they can turn to obtain knowledge or ideas over the years.

5. *They are strong communicators and exceptional listeners.* They listen to their people and recognize that the men and women, who although not in leadership positions themselves can contribute ideas and suggestions that may be even more valuable than his or her own. The good leader establishes cooperative, collaborative climates in which all participants know their participation in decisions are welcome.

6. *They are flexible under pressure and keep their emotions in check.* When faced with failure, their commitment keeps them from succumbing to defeat. In Chapter 1, we discussed how to regain self-confidence after suffering from defeat. Good leaders follow these advice. They will not let failures or disappointments keep them from continuing to try and to encourage their followers to move forward.

7. *They have positive attitudes.* The practice of positive thinking increases our ability tremendously, for two reasons. First, because it discovers ability which was locked up before, calls out hitherto unknown resources; and second, it keeps our minds in harmony by killing fear, worry, anxiety, destroying all the enemies of our success and efficiency. It puts our minds in a condition to succeed. It sharpens our faculties, makes them keener, because it gives a new outlook upon life;

and turns us about so that we face towards our goal, towards certainty, towards assurance, instead of towards doubt, fear and uncertainty. We must accentuate the positive in our thoughts and actions. If we are positive thinkers, our associates will most likely be positive thinkers.

8. *They nurture the cooperation and collaboration of their team.* Good leaders aren't complacent. They're constantly on the lookout for making innovations that will improve the way work is done, assure continuing customer satisfaction, and increase the profitability of the organization.

9. *Their minds are open to new ideas and they welcome suggestions.* Even after changes and improvements are made, they still look for even better ways to accomplish their goals. They take the time to get to know what drives individual team members and enjoy motivating and helping them to succeed. Great leaders understand people—what causes them to act and react the way they do.

10. *They recognize the importance of being a motivating factor for people—appealing to the drives and the feelings of others.* They take a genuine interest in the people with whom they interact. As Dale Carnegie succinctly pointed out: "You can make more friends in two months by becoming genuinely interested in others than you can in two years by trying to get others interested in you."

11. *They recognize and maximize strengths in others.* Often people in positions of authority can compel subordinates to follow orders by dint of the power of their jobs. But such people are not true leaders. Yes, the orders will be followed but

that is all that will happen. True leaders develop confidence and trust in their associates (Note they think of them as associates—not subordinates). This engenders a desire not only to follow the lead of the manager, but also to initiate, innovate, and implement ideas of their own that fit into the established goals.

12. *They hold themselves and others accountable for results.* They set standards, which are understood and accepted by their associates, and work to meet those standards. They take immediate action to correct deviations. They recognize their own limitations and seek help when needed.

13. *They are efficient and manage their time effectively.* They develop meaningful time schedules, learn to prioritize, and to minimize interruptions and distractions.

14. *They are creative and innovative.* They are not afraid to try new ideas. Good leaders aren't complacent. They're constantly on the alert for making innovations that will improve the way work is done, assure continuing customer satisfaction and increase the profitability of the organization. Their minds are open to new ideas and they welcome suggestions. Even after changes and improvements are made, they still look for even better ways to accomplish their goals.

15. *They have vision.* Great leaders know what they want to accomplish and what steps they must take to achieve their goals. They look beyond meeting short-term objectives and keep the big picture clearly in their minds. Theodore Hesburgh, former president, Notre Dame University, expressed this succinctly: "The very essence of leadership is that you have to have vision.

It's got to be a vision you articulate clearly and forcefully on every occasion. You can't blow an uncertain trumpet."

16. *They Focus on Getting Things Done.* We've all come across people in management positions who appear to have great attributes of leadership, but somehow never quite succeed. Somewhere along the line they have missed the boat.

Here is an example: When the ABC Distributing Co. hired Brian as a regional sales manager, they were extremely enthusiastic about him. He had come to them highly recommended. During the selection process, he had impressed the Marketing Manager with his thorough knowledge of their markets, his innovative ideas on how to increase business and his charming personality. During the first several months on the job, he developed a creative and comprehensive marketing program for his region. He spent weeks fine-tuning, writing materials, and creating graphics for it. This led to his making several impressive presentations to management and to the sales force. And that's where it ended. He was never able to actually go out and make the program work. When the Marketing Manager checked back with his previous employer, he learned that Brian had been a staff marketer—brilliant in that type of work—but he had never had line responsibility. He lacked that key ingredient of leadership—getting things done.

17. *They are not easily deterred.* When faced with failure they take the reins and fight to overcome the problem. A good example is Tom Monaghan, founder of Domino's Pizza. He grew this company from a one-store pizza parlor to a chain of several thousand home-delivery outlets over a period of about 30 years. In 1989, he sold the company. After two and

a half years, the company that had purchased the chain lost the momentum Monaghan had generated. In order to save the company, he bought back the company and returned to his former position as CEO. He revitalized the company and expanded it to over 5000 stores in the United States, and over 3000 in other countries.

Transitioning from Doing to Leading

One of the main reasons people are promoted into management and leadership positions is because they were effective at what they did in their jobs. When you get that promotion, your job is to get others to be able to do things as well as or better than you did them. These require a totally different skill set. The success requires making the transition from doing to leading in order to leverage our skills and our time.

Balancing People and Process

To be effective as a manager one must balance people and process. Being too people focused may result in situations where if a key person leaves, everything stops. Being too process focused means that great systems are in place, however no one understands them or wants to work within them. Process focus says: "Here's the plan and here's how we do things." People focus says: "Let's discuss the plan and why we do things." With the right balance, both productivity and commitment stay at their highest levels.

Balancing Motivation and Accountability

Without motivation nothing gets done but some people believe that as soon as we try to hold people accountable they get demotivated. This is not necessarily so. We can develop tools to hold people accountable for their goals, objectives, and commitments and stay motivated at the same time. With this balance, we have more control over the results for ourselves and our team.

If you do not like people generally, there is one simple way of cultivating the characteristic—just look for the good traits, you'll be sure to find some.

Dale Carnegie

Communicating and Coaching for Results

Today, more than ever, a manager's job is to build people. When we can create an environment where people get results, develop new skills, and become successful, we are fulfilling our highest calling as a manager and a leader of people. Communicating with strength and sensitivity, being a coach, and building people are a leader's highest priority.

One of the reasons people are often promoted to manager is because they have demonstrated the skills and knowledge necessary to excel in their area of expertise. Now, success depends not on personal achievement, but coaching others to succeed. Successfully transitioning from worker to manager demands a new frame of mind and set of skills.

Setting Goals and Planning to Achieve Them

The first step we must take in applying our leadership skills is to set goals. Like a good navigator, the effective leader determines what goals should be set and how and when to reach those goals.

Some people prefer the term "objectives". Goals and objectives are interchangeable terms that describe the purpose, or long-term results, toward which an organization's or individual's endeavors are directed.

There are people who like to set out on a journey without a map. They want to ride the currents, and hope that they'll find adventure and fortune—and sometimes they do—but leaders and managers in companies and other organizations can't afford to take those risks because they have responsibilities to their teams. They must know where they want to go, what they want to accomplish, what kinds of problems they may encounter along the way, and how to overcome those problems.

Unless we know exactly what we want to achieve, there's no way to measure how close we are to achieving it. Specific goals give us a standard against which to measure our progress.

The goals we set for accomplishing our team's mission must be in line with what the larger goals our organization sets for us. If we don't coordinate the objectives of what we plan to achieve for our job, department, or team with the objectives of the organization, we will be wasting our time and energy.

Goals are the foundation of motivational programs. In striving to reach our goals, we become motivated. In knowing the goals of our team members and helping them reach those goals, we help to motivate them.

In most organizations, overall big-picture goals are established by top management and filtered down to departments or teams, who use them as guides in establishing their own goals.

The Goal Setting Process

The process of setting goals takes time, energy, and effort. Goals aren't something we scribble on a napkin during our coffee break. We must plan what we truly want to accomplish, establish timetables, determine who will be responsible for which aspect of the job, and then anticipate and plan a resolution for any obstacles that may threaten to thwart the achievement of our goals.

Goals must be spelled out. They must be fully understood by all those who have to meet them. The managers—whether in the top echelon or in any other level of the management hierarchy—must not only be aware of the company's goals, but must be fully committed to them.

Benefits of Establishing Goals

> Establishing goals helps motivate the individuals who are performing the tasks. If people know why something is required they are more likely to learn to do it well and so accomplish the purpose than if they are just told to do it. People take pride in doing a good job. Unless they know the objectives of the job they are doing, they cannot really know whether they are doing satisfactory work or not.
>
> For example, Neil, an engineering student, was in a cooperative education program in which he worked three months in industry and attended classes for three months. His job was in a research laboratory of a large plastics company, where he was assigned a routine testing job. The work was repetitive and dull; Neil soon lost interest in it, and his performance fell. The laboratory manager, seeing the

effect on the work, took Neil aside and carefully explained the importance of testing, the use of the results and exactly how the work contributed to meeting the company's goal of producing a superb product. Once Neil understood the nature of the efforts he was making, his performance improved and he was soon producing top level results.

> Establishing goals provides consistence in planning. When several persons are engaged in making the plans for an organization, a thorough understanding of the goals will make it easier to develop plans that are in line with the overall objectives. Each person involved in the planning process keeps an eye on the major goals and fits his or her aspect of the planning into the whole picture.

> Establishing goals provides a sound basis for coordination and control. On the basis of these goals, performance standards can be set and these in turn become guideposts against which actual performance can be measured.

Build in Flexibility

Sometimes we just can't reach a goal. Circumstances may change. What once seemed to be viable may no longer be. Instead of becoming frustrated, we should be flexible.

Changing Goals with Changing Circumstances

All of us set goals based on certain circumstances we anticipate during the life of a project. Circumstances do change however, and original goals may have to be adjusted. To anticipate that end, many companies use a goal-setting program that involves three levels:

- ➤ Alternative 1: A main, or standard goal: What we plan to accomplish if everything goes well.
- ➤ Alternative 2: A slightly lower goal: If circumstances change and it becomes obvious that our main goal cannot be achieved, rather than starting from scratch in redefining our goal, we can shift to this alternative.
- ➤ Alternative 3: A higher-level goal: If we're making greater progress than we had originally thought we could, rather than being complacent about being ahead of target, shift to this alternative and accomplish even more.

Take, for example, PCX, a company in the metropolitan Philadelphia area that services and repairs computers. Its sales goal for one year was to open ten new accounts. To prevent loss of customers when a national competitor opened a service outlet in the same community, all the company's energies were redirected toward saving its current accounts. The goal of attracting new clients then had to be reduced.

On the other hand, if PCX was having a good year, its goals could have been accelerated. If PCX had gained eight new clients in the first half of the year, it could have automatically raised its goal to a higher level.

Getting the Team to Buy into the Goal-Setting Process

At a recent goal-setting seminar, one participant complained: "I have trouble getting people to buy in to the big picture concept. They're so absorbed in their individual jobs that they can't see beyond their own problems."

Here's how we can overcome this type of situation:

> Bring everyone in the department or on our project team into the early stages of the planning process.
> Discuss the major points of the overall plan.
> Ask each person to describe how he or she will fit in to the big-picture plan.

> Give each person a chance to comment on each stage of the project. Breaking a long-term goal into bite-size pieces that people can relate to can help them to see how their part in a project fits together with the other parts. They can also then see how to set overall team or project goals for the long-run.

> Become thoroughly familiar with each of the team member's goals. If their goals aren't in line with those of the company, department, or project group, demonstrate to them how applying their skills to meeting the team's goals enhances the opportunity to fulfill their own expectations.

The Planning Process

The entire team should be involved in developing the team's plans for each project or assignment. As supervisor or team leader, we should coordinate and lead the process. Assign particular aspects of the planning to the associates who are the most knowledgeable about them, coordinate the process, and make decisions that have a significant effect on the entire project.

Planning must be tied in with the organization's goals. Unless one adheres to these goals, planning will be haphazard. Once the goals are clearly defined, the planners must diagnose the problems that the plan is to cover. To do this certain steps should be followed:

> *Clarify the problem.* Make sure that each of the planners understand the problem in the same way. For example, if the objective of an overall plan is to increase sales, and one participant diagnoses the situation as problem in better sales techniques, while another sees it as a problem in pricing, no solution can be reached. To assure that the situation is clearly understood by all planners, ask these questions:

> *What must be done*? Is it to correct inefficiency? To prepare for contingencies? To change a method? Or some specific matter?

> *Why must it be done?* If it is not done, what will happen? Is the action essential to solve present problems or to prepare for the future? How will this action affect company goals?

> *When should it be done?* Is there an emergency? If not, what time-table should be established to accomplish it?

> *Where will it take place?* Are facilities available for the plan and its implementation?

> *Who will be assigned to develop the plan?* Will it be assigned to a special planning group or to the staff members who are engaged in the current operation and will be responsible for implementing it?

> *How will it be done?* In what manner will the plan be made and later implemented?

SOPs: The Company Bible

One frequently used type of planning is the establishment of Standard Operating Procedures (SOPs), sometimes called Standard Practices (SPs), that details the organization's plans and policies. Although progressive organizations usually restrict their SOPs to such matters as personnel policies, safety measures, and related matters. Many companies, however, either incorporate specific job methods and procedures into their "Bibles" or publish them in accompanying "instruction manuals." Providing policies and procedures for routine activities eliminates the need to plan anew for them every time they occur. Because SOPs set standards that everyone must follow, all employees working with the manuals can refer to them at any time, which ensures consistency in dealing with particular situations.

If we have to develop SOPs, keep them simple. SOPs too often become complicated because of manager's desires to cover every possible contingency. It can't be done. Managers will frequently have to make decisions based on many unforeseeable factors. SOPs should cover the common issues in detail, but leave room for managers (or non-managerial people, where appropriate) to make spontaneous decisions when circumstances warrant them.

SOPs should also be flexible. Don't make SOPs so rigid that they can't be changed when circumstances change. Plans may become obsolete because of new technologies, competition, government regulations, or the development of more efficient methods. Build into SOPs a policy for periodic review and adjustment.

Also keep in mind that not all plans are SOPs. Plans may be developed for special purposes, sometimes to be used only once, and sometimes for projects that last several months or even years.

Standard Operating Procedures are just one phase of planning. As mentioned, it's best if SOPs should cover only broad policy matters so that specific plans can be designed for new projects as they're created.

A Guide to Successful SOPs:

> Clearly state what actions are expected from each participant.
> Specify where deviations may be allowed and when they are not permitted.
> Test the SOP before making it final.

Obstacles to Enforcing Accountability

No matter how well our plans are designed, there are likely to be challenges from associates or other managers. Our results, and the results of our team, depend on how those situations are handled. Fairness, consistency, and strength are required in the right places, at the right time, and in the right way. Without this, morale can grind to a low for everyone, effecting productivity, customer loyalty, and employee loyalty—all mandatory in today's highly competitive work force. Here are some suggestions to deal with this:

> Make sure that all goals and objectives are clear and communicated to everybody involved and that they not only understand but accept them.
> Performance objectives should be clearly indicated. How this can be done will be discussed in chapter 5.
> Goals and standards should not be revised unless serious problems change the scope of the project.
> Assure that all stake holders buy into, and feel a sense of ownership of the goals and standards. Milestones and methods of measuring, monitoring, and communicating achievements are determined.
> Encourage associates to ask the right questions to uncover barriers to achieving results.

- Set and adhere to time schedules.
- Provide coaching and feedback techniques.
- Be aware of lack of motivation and burnout of those involved in the project and take action to overcome it.
- Establish relevant reward system for achievement of goals.

Principles for Holding Ourselves and Others Accountable

We, as leaders of our teams are primarily accountable for its success or failure. To assure success we have the obligation to see that our associates recognize that they too are accountable. Here are some guidelines to help in this:

- Make immediate, intermediate, and long-term goals.
- Align performance objectives with corporate strategy.
- Be aware of changes in the scope of the project and revise goals, procedures, and deadlines, if plans or projects change.
- Gain agreement and buy-in on established goals and standards.
- Consistently broadcast established goals, objectives, checkpoints, and milestones to all involved.
- Ask the right questions, confront challenges head-on, and seek input to eliminate barriers to reaching goals.
- Prioritize activities, stay focused, and manage time according to performance goals.
- Set up a mentor system and learn ways to effectively coach and give constructive feedback.
- Maintain enthusiasm, commitment, and motivation by giving sincere and consistent recognition.
- Develop a relevant reward system for the achievement of goals.

Sum and Substance

Effective leaders follow these principles:

- › Team members respond better to participatory, rather than authoritarian leadership.
- › Associates should be given every opportunity to use their talents, skills, and brainpower.
- › The good leader establishes a cooperative, collaborative climate in which all participants know their participation in decisions are welcome.
- › Good leaders think of themselves as facilitators. Their job is to make it easy for their associates to accomplish their jobs.
- › Effective leaders are ready to take the initiative, to act rather than react.
- › The best leaders set high standards for themselves and then work hard to achieve their goals.
- › They focus on getting things done and are not easily deterred.

3

MOTIVATING OUR STAFFS

As our people report to work have we ever asked ourselves, "Are they happy to be here? Would they rather be working for somebody else? Is it just the salary we pay them or the benefits our company provides that motivate them to come to work?" These are important, but most companies today pay satisfactory salaries and offer comparable benefits packages. It has to be more than that. Psychologists tell us that there are five basic motivating factors in a person's relationship to his or her job.

Recognition as an Individual

Each of our people is different from us and from the other people in the group. Each person likes to feel that we recognize these differences and treat him or her as a special person not as an interchangeable standard part. Supervisors must listen and observe the people they supervise and learn to differentiate among them. Learn their strengths and limitations, their likes and dislikes, how they act and react and tailor the way we deal with each of their individualities.

By paying attention to these differences we learn that each has one or more special concerns about his or her job. We find that Joe is highly security conscious and will take no risks for fear of failing and maybe jeopardizing his job. We note that Betty is very ambitious and wants to move up as fast as she can. Among our other people, Sam and Lil need constant reassurance while Karen is always trying new approaches. By keeping these individual differences in mind, we will be able to work most effectively with each of them and help them obtain what they want most from us as their managers.

Pride in Work

Most people who have reached supervisory or management positions take pride in their jobs. They usually have earned the promotion and have significant accomplishments in their work. These men and women are considered an important part of the company. If we can instill this sense of pride in *all* our people, it will lead to higher morale and commitment.

To accomplish this each new employee should be given a thorough orientation on what the department does and how it relates to overall company activities. He or she should also be told how the specific job performed helps the department and the company accomplishes its mission.

Appreciation and praise should be given whenever appropriate. Dale Carnegie encouraged us to be "hearty in our approbation and lavish in our praise." When people know that their work is appreciated, a sense of pride develops, and is maintained.

Sense of Belonging

Many organizations boast of the *esprit de corps* that they generate. Team spirit is essential to successful group activity. People like to feel that they are a part of something bigger than themselves: a team, a social group, a military unit or a company. These feelings flow directly from pride in one's job, but that is only the beginning. People are happier, more cooperative, and productive when they identify with their group—especially a successful and effective group. People brag about having served in the U.S. Marine Corps long after their service has been completed. People proudly tell others they are employed by IBM, AT&T, Sony, Toyota or other prestigious companies.

How can we build this feeling of belonging in our people? Good managers build team spirit by keeping objectives clearly in front of their people and getting their people to participate in determining how they will meet these objectives. By getting people involved in decisions which affect their work, they feel that they are important to the department and this solidifies their commitment. If they are enthusiastic about the job, they will be motivated to do their best.

Flaming enthusiasm, backed up by horse sense and persistence, is the quality that most frequently makes for success.

Dale Carnegie

Fair Treatment

Policies and procedures should be established, clearly communicated to the employees, and administered in a consistent manner. Cindy and Sandy both have tardiness problems. The boss likes Cindy and is not too fond of Sandy. She enforces the disciplinary action for tardiness for Sandy, but lets Cindy get away with a light reprimand. Not only will Sandy be upset, but the other people in the department will consider this unfair. People who commit the same offenses should receive the same treatment.

People respond emotionally—not rationally—when their self-interest is in jeopardy. The desire for fair treatment is deep seated in the emotional makeup of all people. Favoritism is the greatest of demoralizers. It destroys the feeling of security in others who fear that their own efforts and worth are not being recognized.

Chance to Express Ideas

Billy never forgot his first boss. "I thought up a great idea that could increase production in my department. All excited, I went to the boss to tell him about it. He never even listened. He said, 'You're paid to work not to think. Go back to your machine.' I never suggested another idea while I was on that job."

People who work on the job have a great deal of insight into the operation and often come up with good suggestions. All of us are more creative than we think we are. We should make a practice to encourage our people to make suggestions and take each one of them seriously. If it is not acceptable, explain why, but never ignore it.

Employees should feel free to discuss their personal progress with their manager. Some supervisors inadvertently erect a barrier between themselves and their people so that associates do not feel comfortable to approach them. We may not realize this, but if our people rarely come to us with their problems, it does not mean that there are none. It is more likely that employees do not feel free to discuss them with us.

What Makes Employees Tick

Let's take another look at some of the factors that employees seek in their jobs:

Recognition and appreciation

As noted above, recognition is a key factor. This was reinforced by a report of The Society for Human Resource Management, based on a Gallup Poll of 400 companies. It confirmed that an employee's relationship with his or her direct boss is more responsible for retention than pay or job perks. Fair and inspiring leadership, including coaching and mentoring, retains employees. Another Gallup Poll revealed that a key indicator of employee satisfaction and productivity is an employee's belief that the boss cares about the employee and can be trusted.

Some people are driven more by other forms of incentives than by money. In a study by Employee Retention Headquarters, appreciation and involvement are cited more than money as what keeps employees happy. They need to be convinced, verbally and nonverbally, that management respects their position and that they are important to the success of their organization. They enjoy celebrating milestones and victories, publicly and privately, verbally and in writing, promptly and sincerely.

Stimulating and fulfilling work

In October 2003, ASTD (*American Society for Training & Development*) newsletter reported that for most workers today, stimulating and valuable work is more important than salary and advancement. It's hard to put a price tag on enthusiasm and excitement for a job. Managers, who foster involvement of employees and include them early on in projects, obtain more creative ideas and create greater employee investment and pride in the outcome. Employees who actively participate in making decisions on a broad spectrum of issues help create an environment that they like and one in which they want to remain.

A clear career path and growth opportunities

By providing opportunities for growth, both personally and professionally, employees are less likely to look elsewhere.

Providing training opportunities with respect to new skill development and career development is an indication that a manager is willing to invest on behalf of the employee. This is critical for employee retention. Encouraging employees to join professional organizations by paying the membership fee and giving employees the time off and admission fees needed to attend lunches and conferences motivates employees. Companies who have a high retention rate hold a reputation for hiring from within. A jointly agreed upon career path will gain the commitment of employees and ensure their acceptance of organizational goals and direction.

Managers who respect a balanced life

Organizations that walk the talk of a balanced life have higher retention than those who believe that the employee should eat, breathe, and sleep work. Acknowledging and respecting the importance of family and personal life of employees prevents burnout and fosters loyalty. According to the Society for Human Resource Management, employers need to be aware of quality of work–life issues. They must be willing to offer flexible schedules and be sensitive to dual careers, childcare, and parent care challenges.

Competitive compensation and benefits

Money is important, but it is less important than we might think. Employees expect to be paid fairly and competitively. They feel entitled to the standard benefits of health insurance and retirement plans. In a survey 92 percent of respondents indicated that a $10,000 annual salary increase would not prompt them to change employers if they were receiving personal and professional development coaching.

Motivating for Peak Performance

Our first job as a manager or leader is to develop the skills and abilities of each of our associates so that they can perform at top capacity. The best way to begin is to learn about each person as an individual.

We may think that all we really have to know about our associates is how well they do their work. Wrong! Knowing the members of our team requires more than just knowing their job skill—that's an important part, but it's only a part of their total make-up. Learn what's important to our associates—their ambitions and goals, their families, their special concerns—in other words, what makes them tick.

Method of Operation

Each of us has our own special way in which we do our work and the way we live our lives. This is our "MO" (Method of Operation). Study the way each of our staff members operates, and we'll discover his or her MO. For example, we might notice that one person always ponders on a subject before commenting on it, and another might reread everything she's worked on several times before starting new work. Being aware of these work styles helps us understand people and enable us to work with them more effectively.

By observing and listening, we can learn a great deal about our colleagues. Listen when they speak to us: listen to what they say, and listen to what they don't say. Listen when they speak to others. Eavesdropping may not be polite, but we can learn a great deal. Observe how our associates do their work and how they act and react. It doesn't take long to identify their likes and dislikes, their quirks and eccentricities. By listening, we can learn about the things that are important to each of them and the "hot buttons" that can turn them on or off.

To get the most from each of our employees, we must understand them as human beings and work with them as individuals to help them make and meet commitments to perform even better than they have up to now.

As noted above, we must recognize that all human beings are not the same and we must deal with each of them according to his or her individuality rather than trying to get them all to do the same thing in the same way. Let's take the word "PEOPLE" and by expanding on each letter obtain some hints on how we can achieve our goal of better performance through our people.

Personality

Each person has his or her own special personality. A manager must take the time to get to know how each of them acts and reacts, what turns them on or off, what really is of concern to them. A major error made by many supervisors is to attempt to treat all people alike. Some people need much more attention than others, while some look upon your attention as prying or condescending. There are people who need constant reinforcement, while others only need an occasional pat on the back.

Exceptional Characteristics

Look for those traits that make each person stand out from the others. Laurie is very creative. In her spare time she draws, sculpts and writes poetry. How can that help on the job? By appealing to her creativity, we can get Laurie to tackle difficult projects or contribute ideas and suggestions that may help solve job problems. Gary is a perfectionist. His work may be slow, but it is always right. By giving him assignments where quality is paramount, we will be utilizing him most effectively.

Opportunity

Claudette's job was basically boring. But her boss recognized that she was anxious to learn and would give her full efforts to her boring job if she could see how it could lead to more challenging work. By giving Claudette opportunity to learn about other jobs in the department, she was able to train and prepare for them; thus encouraging her to learn and grow.

Opportunity is not limited to possible advancement on the job. There are people who do not want the responsibility of supervisory or management jobs, but seek opportunities to expand their knowledge or perform work that is of more interest to them. David considered himself a "people-person." He relates well to other people, but in his job as an accountant he spends most of his time working by himself. By giving David the opportunity to train others in the department in various company procedures and to periodically conduct department meetings, his enthusiasm for the job increased and his overall performance was enhanced.

Participation

People who work on a job have a lot more insight into how a job should be done than we may realize. When a new procedure has to be developed or a new project planned, have the people who will do the job participate in determining how it should be done. As the manager of the department, Kathy believed she knew exactly how the new project should be planned. After all she had years of experience in this work. However, instead of designing the plan and then telling her people how it would be done, she brought them into the early stages of the planning procedure. Not only did they come up with some excellent ideas that Kathy had not considered, but because they were participants in the planning, they felt committed to work hard to assure it would succeed.

Leadership

Good leaders do not set goals for their people and tell them how to reach them. Good leaders work with their people to encourage them to set their own goals and give them the tools they need to reach them.

Fred was an intelligent man and a good worker, but Paul, his boss, felt he had much more capability than he was using. Fred was afraid to take the initiative on any project and continually came to Paul for instructions. To help Fred overcome this, Paul began giving Fred small projects and made him responsible for their completion. By gradually increasing the complexity of these assignments, Paul helped Fred develop the self-confidence he needed to really give an outstanding performance.

Expectations

Let people know that we expect high performance. Do not be satisfied with mediocre work. Too many managers are delighted if their people meet minimum standards. This may be OK if business is flourishing, but when companies have to fight to stay alive, we need more than just meeting standards. Our people must be encouraged to try to keep getting better and better.

Rewards for achieving goals often help. Mary Kay Ash, the founder of the Mary Kay cosmetics company, attributes the

great success of her company to her practice of having her people keep setting higher and higher expectations for themselves—and then by rewarding them with some form of recognition when those goals are met.

When people are expected by their bosses, by their families and most important by themselves to keep improving their performance, nothing can stop them from becoming real achievers.

By knowing our people and working with them, and utilizing their individual strengths will result in the collective efficacy of our department and higher performance for the organization.

Money as a Motivator

Here's a mini-lesson in logic:

A: The more money we earn, the happier we are.
B: The more work we produce, the more money we earn. Therefore:
C: People will stretch to produce more, earn more and thereby will become happier.

But is it true? Sometimes, but not always. Assume A and B are both true, it should logically follow that C is true. Right? Sometimes it is, but often it is not.

Let's look into why money is not always the motivator that it logically appears to be.

Motivators versus Satisfiers

A team of behavioral scientists led by Frederick Herzberg studied what people want from their jobs and classified the results into two categories:

1. *Satisfiers* (also called maintenance factors): Factors people require from a job to justify minimum effort. These factors include working conditions, money, and benefits. After employees are satisfied, however, just giving them more of the same factors will not motivate them to work harder. Many of what most people consider motivators are really just satisfiers.
2. *Motivators*: Factors that stimulate people to put out more

energy, effort, and enthusiasm in their job. They make them really move.

To see how this concept works on the job, suppose that we work in a less-than-adequate facility, in which lighting is poor, ventilation is inadequate, and space is tight. Productivity, of course, is low.

In a few months, our company moves to new quarters, with excellent lighting and air-conditioning and lots of space, and productivity shoots up.

The company CEO is elated. He says to the board of directors, "I've found the solution to high productivity: If we give people better working conditions, they'll produce more, so I'm going to make the working conditions even better." He hires an interior designer, has new carpet installed, hangs paintings on the walls, and places plants around the office. The employees are delighted. It's a pleasure to work in these surroundings—but productivity doesn't increase at all.

Why not? People seek a level of satisfaction in their job—in this case, reasonably good working conditions. When the working environment was made acceptable, employees were satisfied, and it showed up in their productivity. After the conditions met their level of satisfaction, however, added enhancements didn't motivate them.

So What Does This Have to Do with Money?

Money, like working conditions, is a satisfier. We might assume that offering more money generates higher productivity. And we're probably right—for most people, but not for everyone. Incentive programs, in which people are given an opportunity to earn more money by producing more, are part of many company compensation plans. They work for some people, but not for others.

The sales department is a good example. Because salespeople usually work on a commission, or incentive basis, they're in the enviable position of rarely having to ask for a raise. If salespeople want to earn more money, all they have to do is work harder or smarter and make as much money as they want. Therefore, all salespeople are very rich. Right? Wrong!

How come this logic doesn't work? Sales managers have complained about this problem from the beginning of time. They say: "We have an excellent incentive program, and the money is there for our sales staff. All they have to do is reach out—and they don't. Why not?"

We have to delve deep into the human psyche for an answer. We all set personal salary levels, consciously or subconsciously, at which we are satisfied. Until we reach that point, money does motivate us, but after that no more. This level varies significantly from person to person.

Some people set this point very high, and money is a major motivator to them; others are content at lower levels. It doesn't mean that they don't want their annual raise or bonus, but if obtaining the extra money requires special effort or inconvenience, we can forget it.

For example, suppose that Derek is in our production group and that his salary is 60 percent of ours. His wife works, but we know by the nature of her job that it doesn't pay much. Derek drives a twelve-year-old car and buys his clothes at thrift shops. The only vacations his family has ever taken are occasional camping trips. We feel sorry for him. But now we can help Derek. We need several workers for a special project to be done over the next six Saturdays at double-time pay. When we ask Derek whether he wants the assignment, he says "No," and we can't understand why. It seems to us that he should be eager to make more money, but he has already reached his level of satisfaction. To him, having the Saturday off to be with his family is more important than the opportunity to earn more money.

This example doesn't mean that money doesn't motivate at all. The opportunity to earn money motivates everyone up to the point that they are satisfied. Some people, like Derek, are content at lower levels. As long as they can meet their basic needs, other things are more important to them than money. To other people, this point is very high, and they extend themselves to keep making more money.

By learning as much as we can about our associates, we learn about their interests, goals, and lifestyles and the level of income at which they're satisfied. To offer the opportunity to make more money as an incentive to people who don't care about it is futile. We have to find some other ways to motivate them.

Benefits: Motivators or Satisfiers?

Benefits are important in most companies. These companies provide some form of health insurance, life insurance, pensions, and other benefits to their employees. In fact, the benefits package is one of the factors that potential employees seek when they evaluate a job offer—but it isn't a motivator. Have we ever known anyone who worked harder because the company introduced a dental-insurance program?

Benefits are satisfiers. Good benefits attract people to work for a company, and they also keep people from quitting.

Keeping employees happy is not enough. The challenge is to develop high performance standards that challenge employees and motivate them to stretch to meet these standards. Some of these motivators are:

Recognition

Human beings crave recognition. People like to know that others know who they are, what they want, and what they believe. Recognition begins when we learn and use people's names. Of course we know the names of the men and women in our work group, but often we will be coordinating work with other groups, with internal and external suppliers, subcontractors, and customers. Everyone has a name; learn the names of those people. Use them. It's the first step to recognize each person's individuality.

Remember that a person's name is to that person the sweetest sound in any language.

Dale Carnegie

Recognition is not limited to using a name. In Warren's exit interview after quitting his job with the Building Maintenance Company, he was asked what he liked most and least about the company. Warren responded that although the salary and benefits were good, he never felt that he was part of the organization. "I always felt that I was looked at as nothing more than a cog in the machine," he said. "During the nine months I worked in the department, I made several suggestions, offered to take on extra projects, and tried to apply creative approaches to some of the work assigned to me. My boss didn't recognize all that I could have contributed."

Show We Care

Just as we have a life outside the company, so do our associates. A job is an important part of our lives, but there are many aspects of life that may be of greater importance: health, family, and outside interests, for example. Show sincere interest in the associate as a total person.

Virginia, the head teller of a savings and loan association in Wichita, Kansas, makes a point of welcoming back associates who have been on vacation or out for several days because of illness. She asks them about their vacation or the state of their health and brings them up-to-date on company news. She makes them feel that she missed them, and it comes across sincerely because she really did miss them.

Jacob, a grandfather, realizes that children are the center of most families. He takes a genuine interest in the activities of his coworkers' children and has even accompanied associates to school events in which their children participate. Some people may consider this situation paternalistic or intrusive, but Jake's true concern comes across as positive interest and has helped meld his team members into a working family.

Praise

Twice I did good and that I heard never. Once I did bad and that I heard ever.

Dale Carnegie

There are supervisors who never praise their people. They rationalize that people are supposed to do good work and need not be praised for doing what is expected of them. One crusty supervisor boasted: "I never praise people. They know they're doing OK if I leave them alone. If I have to talk to them, they're in trouble."

Human beings crave praise. We all want to know that other people recognize our accomplishments and achievements. This is especially important when the praise is from our supervisor or other people whom we respect.

Praise Must Be Sincere

Carol was about to leave the room to attend a meeting. She paused when she reached the door, turned around and said: "Gang, I want to let we know you're doing a great job," smiled and left the room. At the meeting she told her colleagues how she boosted the morale of her department by her parting remark. Back in her department, her people looked upon it quite differently. One of the men loudly commented to the others: "She's just given us her monthly positive reinforcement."

What Carol assumed to be a morale builder was perceived by her people to be insincere. Praise must be sincere and we can't fake sincerity.

One way to make praise truly sincere is to incorporate the reason for the praise into the praise itself. Instead of saying: "Good job, Joe," it is far more effective to say "Joe, the way you handled that customer complaint is a fine example of the professionalism we like to see in this department."

Combining Criticism With Praise

When an employee has to be criticized, many supervisors sandwich the criticism between praise. This is supposed to make the criticism more palatable. Often this does reduce the resentment which often accompanies censure. However, if the only praise given is always accompanied by some form of negative comments, the praise becomes meaningless. When the supervisor begins the praise, the employee is thinking: "OK, when does he throw it at me?"

Typically, the conversation goes: "Sam, you are one of our fastest workers and I appreciate that, *but* you make too many errors...." The minute Sam hears that word "but," his mind blocks out the praise. He knows the next words will be criticism.

Barry overcomes this by substituting "and" for "but:" "Sam, you are one of our fastest workers. I appreciate that, *and* you could become even more effective if you improved the quality of the work. Let's see what we can do together to help you in that."

The word "and" does not have the negative connotation of "but." The employee still retains the glow of the praise and is open to suggestions for improvement.

Fear of Praising

Some managers comment, "If I praise workers who are doing well more often than others, won't this be considered favoritism?"

Not necessarily. When recognition is clearly deserved, and extended to everybody who deserves it, this is not favoritism. Those who are not praised should realize that they have not earned it.

Another concern: "When a person's performance improves significantly, is it better to give them extra praise than somebody who has done good work all along?"

Excessive praise can arouse resentment in those who have always been performing in a desirable way. Also excessive recognition can convey the idea that we expect exceptional achievement to become routine. We must tailor the way we praise to the needs of the specific associate.

When that person reaches the standard that is expected, praise him or her for the accomplishment and point out that this is what the other good workers are doing and we appreciate it. Do this in front of co-workers, so all know that this praise is based on reaching this level and is not for exceptional work. Naturally, persons who still do better should receive special recognition.

Managers ask: "Should people be praised for performing average work consistently?" Everybody needs praise, but to give special recognition for routine performance is self-defeating. It gives the person no incentive to improve. Occasionally, the supervisor might compliment them on some special achievement or comment on their good attendance record. This should not be done on a regular basis or it loses its value. Praise should never be given on a schedule. "Today is the 14th, it's my day to praise Kathy," but given at a time when the circumstances warrant it.

Communicating Praise

Be immediate: The best time to praise is at the time the praiseworthy event occurs. When Alice presented her report to her boss, he immediately complimented her on completing it before the deadline. After he read it, he again praised her for its content.

Be specific: As mentioned earlier, incorporate what we are praising the person for with the praise itself.

Describe its value to the organization: "By beating that deadline, it enabled us to complete that project and solve our customer's problem to his satisfaction."

Encourage them to keep up the good work: "We have made great progress on this job and I know we will continue to use our excellent skills in helping us achieve our goals."

Five Tips for Effective Praise

As important as praise is in motivating people, it doesn't always work. Some supervisors praise every minor activity, diminishing the value of praise for real accomplishments. Others deliver praise in such a way that it seems phony. To make praise more meaningful, follow these suggestions:

1. Don't overdo it. Praise is sweet. Candy is sweet too, but the more we eat, the less sweet each piece becomes—and we may get a stomachache. Too much praise reduces the benefit that's derived from each bit of praise; if it's overdone, it loses its value altogether.
2. Be sincere. We can't fake sincerity. We must truly believe that what we're praising our associate for is actually commendable. If we don't believe it ourselves, neither will our associate.
3. Be specific about the reason for the praise. Rather than say, "Great job!" it's much better to say, "The report you

wrote on the XYZ matter enabled me to understand more clearly the complexities of the issue."

4. Ask for our associates' advice. Nothing is more flattering than to be asked for advice about how to handle a situation. Caution: This approach can backfire if we don't take the advice. If we have to reject an advice, ask the person questions about their suggestion until they see its limitations and rethink it.

5. Publicize praise. Just as a reprimand should always be given in private, praising should be done (whenever possible) in public. Sometimes the matter for which praise is given is a private issue, but it's more often appropriate to let the entire team in on the praise. If other team members are aware of the praise we give a colleague, it spurs them to work for similar recognition. In some cases, praise for significant accomplishments can be more widely publicized, such as when it's given at meetings or company events.

Give Them Something to Keep

Telling people that we appreciate what they've done is a great idea, but writing it is even more effective. The aura of oral praise fades away; a letter or even a brief note endures. We don't have to spend much money. It doesn't take much time.

Write Thank-You Cards

At the A&G Merchandising Company in Wilmington, Delaware, team leaders are given packets of "thank-you" cards on which the words *Thank You* are printed in beautiful script on the front flap, and the inside of the card is left blank. Whenever someone does something worthy of special recognition, that person's manager writes a note on one of the cards detailing the special accomplishment and congratulating the employee for achieving it. The recipients cherish the cards and show them to friends and family.

Plaques and Certificates

No matter what type of award we give to employees—large or small (cash, merchandise, tickets to a show or sports event, or a trip to a resort, for example)—it's worth spending a few more dollars to include a certificate or plaque. Employees love to hang these mementos in their cubicles or offices, over their workbenches, or in their homes. The cash gets spent, the merchandise wears out, the trip becomes a long-past memory, but a certificate or plaque is a permanent reminder of the recognition.

Motivating Marginal Workers

Who are our marginal workers? These are the people who meet our minimum performance standards, but rarely exceed them. They are not bad enough to be fired, but do not really carry their own weight. Motivating such people is a major challenge to leaders. What are some of the reasons we have marginal workers in our organizations?

Poor Selection

Debbie, a data entry clerk, is a marginal worker. Because data entry clerks were in short supply. Her boss Barbara, hired Debbie even though she did not quite meet the job requirements. Although she was still below the expected performance standard when she completed her probationary period, Barbara decided to keep her. "At least somebody is operating that computer," she rationalized, "and I'll keep working with her and make her productive."

Six months later, despite additional training and coaching, Debbie is still just barely meeting production standards. She does not have the innate capability to be truly productive.

Poor selection is one of the major reasons for marginal production. By establishing realistic job specifications and not compromising when hiring people—even when desperate to fill the job—the chances of selecting people who will succeed on the job will be enhanced.

However, no matter how good our selection procedures may be, errors may be made and the person hired may not make the grade. That is why probationary periods are so important. During this period, the supervisor should make sure the new worker knows what he or she is expected to do and the standards that must be met. Every effort should be made to help this person meet these standards through training, coaching, and special attention.

Be patient. Sometimes the reason for marginal production is not incapability but a lack of understanding or what is to be done. In designing a training program for new people, set specific standards and time tables. Make sure that the trainee is aware of them. If standards are not met at the specified time, we should work with the trainee to overcome the problems that may have caused this.

Every effort should be made to salvage the trainee, but if it fails, do not keep a person who barely meets minimum standards. Once probation is completed, it is much more difficult to terminate a marginal worker.

Good Workers Whose Performance Declines

Phil has been with the company for six years. His production has always been well above the minimum standard and his supervisor, Lil, looked upon him as one of her best people. A few months ago Phil's production began to decline. He seemed to have lost interest in the job.

Why does this happen to people like Phil? Sometimes it's due to personal problems. One's personal life and job life cannot be separated. If there are serious problems at home, it will affect our work.

Sometimes it's due to a real or perceived grievance. Some people keep their grievances deep inside themselves and it festers unless it is brought out and addressed.

In her discussion with Phil, Lil learned that Phil had set certain goals for himself which were not being met on the job. Although his work was praised and his reviews excellent, he had not reached the position he had hoped to reach at this stage of his career.

The supervisor should know the goals of his or her people and do what can be done to help them reach them. Let the worker know what he or she must do to attain the goals—including maintaining a high performance level, taking additional training on the job or through outside study, and pointing out how long it might take to achieve this. If it is not possible for the worker to meet his or her goals on this job, the supervisor and worker together should determine how the goals might be modified so that they could be met on this job.

Boredom

For years Ann was one of the best performers in her department. But now Ann was bored. She had been doing the same job for so long that she no longer enjoyed doing it. She found every excuse to take time off. When she was on the job, she gossiped with her co-workers, extended her breaks, and put out as little production as she could get away with.

One way a supervisor can help formerly productive workers return to productivity is to enrich the job by combining functions that were performed by several people into one job so that each worker does more diverse work. Another is to restructure the manner in which the work is done. This is achieved most effectively when the worker participates in the restructuring. People who work on a job can often come up with ideas to make the work more interesting and effective. Another approach to relieve boredom is to assign the worker special projects. Change of pace is a good antidote to boredom.

Coasters

Michael has been with the company for 22 years and in his present position for eight years. He's happy in his work, but also recognizes that due to the nature of his work and the organizational structure of the company, it is unlikely he will ever be promoted. His work is good; he knows he will never be fired unless he does something drastic, so consciously or subconsciously he decided that there is no point knocking himself out on the job. He'll just coast along until retirement.

Most companies have their share of such "coasters." They are good workers and can contribute to productivity, but they feel they've done their part. How can we remotivate such people?

Associated Products uses "coasters" for new product testing. When they are ready to introduce a new line, they test market it in key cities. Instead of using a test marketing company, they assign this to some of their "old-timers." By being involved in a new and important role shows them they are respected and it gives them an opportunity to do something new and different. This stimulation carries over when they return to their regular work.

Other companies have used these long-term workers as trainers and mentors of new people. Giving them this type of responsibility makes them more dedicated to the job and the company, and can convert them from marginal workers to productive members of the company team.

"My people couldn't care less about their jobs. If I don't keep pushing them, nothing will be accomplished," sighed Al.

"I don't have that problem at all," Carl responded. "My gang is always willing to put forth whatever effort is needed to get the job done."

What is the reason for these diametrically opposite attitudes of the workers that each of these managers supervise? Why is Carl's group so much more highly motivated than Al's? It could be the management style of the supervisor or it could be the work itself.

Behavioral scientists generally agree that although employee motivation is enhanced by such factors as recognition, appreciation, challenge and, of course, fair treatment, the most effective motivator of all is the work itself. If Al's people find their jobs boring and unchallenging, no matter how good a supervisor Al may be, he will have a tough time motivating them. On the other hand, if Carl's people enjoy their work so much that they can't wait to come in every morning and hate to leave each evening, there is little else Carl needs to do to keep them motivated.

Enrich the Job

Unfortunately, a great percentage of jobs in industry today are merely routine, and it is difficult, if not impossible, to generate excitement about them. One way to overcome this is to enrich the job.

When Jennifer was hired to head the claims processing department of the Liability Insurance Company, she inherited a department with low morale, manifested with high turnover, absenteeism, and disgruntled employees. The claims processing operation was an "assembly line." Each clerk checked a section of the claims form, passed it to the next clerk, who checked the next section, and so on. If an error or question of interpretation was discovered, it was put aside for handling by a specialist. From an operational viewpoint, this was highly efficient. However, it made the work dull and unchallenging. Jennifer reorganized the system. She enriched the job by eliminating the "assembly line." Each clerk checked the entire form, corrected errors and sought interpretations. This required added training and did slow the work down in the beginning, but it paid off in developing a highly motivated team of workers who were really interested in their jobs. Turnover, absenteeism and dissatisfaction were significantly reduced, and once the system was fully established, speed and accuracy were increased.

Get the Staff Involved

Engendering an attitude that the job to be done is mutual effort of management and labor, not "superiors" ordering "inferiors" to perform a task—will make the work more interesting and the people engaged in that work more highly motivated to accomplish the job.

When productivity expected is quantifiable, many companies establish production quotas for their workers. This is particularly true in sales and many manufacturing and office positions. Denise heads the Word Processing Section of her company. She has established specific quotas for most of her mass-mailing projects and can measure how well her people are doing by how close they come to meeting the quotas. Denise noted that even her best workers rarely would produce more than the quota. When she tried to increase the number of letters expected, she was faced with resentment and even overt opposition.

When a new project was being planned, instead of superimposing a quota for the project, Denise asked the people who would work on it to study the project. Managers and the workers together should establish quotas or goals that are attainable and acceptable by both. When a person has participated in establishing quotas, that person will feel committed to meet that quota and will willingly work to assure that it is met.

In his book, *How to Win Friends and Influence People*, Dale Carnegie anticipated what the behavioral scientists later promulgated. He wrote: "No one likes to feel that he or she is being sold something or told to do a thing. We much prefer to feel we are buying of our own accord or acting on our own ideas. We like to be consulted about our wishes, our wants, and our thoughts."

The One Best Motivator

Behavioral scientists generally agree that although employee motivation is enhanced by such factors as recognition, appreciation, challenge and, of course, fair treatment, the most effective motivator of all is the work itself. Work can become repetitious, boring, and unchallenging. Some ways to overcome this is redesign jobs to provide diversity, challenge and commitment.

Bring associates into the planning stages of new jobs. Get their input as to production or sales quotas, methods and performance standards. When people feel they "own" the job, they are more likely to put in all their efforts to achieve the goal.

Sum and Substance

Eight ways to give people what they want from their jobs

1. Let each person know how he or she is getting along.
2. Help them improve by coaching and guidance.
3. Be hearty in our approbation and lavish in our praise.
4. Tell people in advance about changes that will affect them and, if possible, why the change is being made.
5. Make the best of each person's ability.
6. Look for ability that is not being used, help that person develop that ability and utilize it.
7. Never block a person's opportunity for advancement.
8. Give people more freedom to control the way they do their jobs. Encourage them to suggest better methods and approaches.

4

....

STAFFING OUR ORGANIZATION

Most managers feel that filling a vacancy in their department is an annoying distraction from their real function. The time, energy and emotional drain that the hiring process involves takes them away from their regular duties, adds extra hours to their day, and worst of all, they fear that they will make the wrong choice and would have to go through the whole process over again in a few months.

In most large companies and in many smaller firms, the human resources department handles recruiting and selecting new employees. However, even when this is done, line supervisors and team leaders have to participate in the process. Almost always, they'll interview prospects. After all, they are the people to whom the person hired will report and they will be responsible for the new employee's success or failure.

In some companies there may not be an H.R. department or, if there is one, it is situated at the home office, so managers at branch facilities are required to do the hiring themselves.

Unfortunately, although these managers are usually skilled in performing work in their own specialty, they don't have the training and experience required for successful hiring. As a result countless errors have occurred—at the minimum, wasted time and effort, and at the worst hiring people who were doomed to fail.

As a supervisor or manager we cannot take this aspect of our job lightly. The men and women we hire will contribute to our success or cause us from meeting our objectives.

Develop Realistic Job Specifications

We can be more effective in selecting the people with whom we will have to work and upon whom we must depend to get the job done by starting the search with a realistic job specification.

Analyze the job carefully and determine just what background the new employee should bring to the job. We should ask ourselves as we list each requirement: "Is this really needed to perform the job?"

Jeff was seeking to fill a job for a customer service representative. One of the specs he established for this job was the requirement of a college degree. Is this realistic? Certainly there are advantages in hiring a college graduate for this job, but does this job really require skills that are acquired in college? Could a person with less formal education do the job just as well?

When Jeff was asked why he wanted a college grad for this job, he responded: "Why not? There are lots of college grads looking for jobs, I might as well take advantage of this and get the best I can." Does this make sense? Requiring more education (or any other qualification) than is really needed has more disadvantages than advantages. Sure, we may get smarter or more creative people, but because these people will not be challenged by the job, they will probably not be as highly productive as persons with less education. People who become bored with the job are the people who become gripers, have high absentee problems, and leave after brief tenures. More important, we may eliminate the best possible candidate for the job by putting the emphasis on the wrong aspect of background.

When Lynn obtained approval to add another accounting clerk to her staff, she told the H.R. department she needed somebody with at least ten years' experience in bookkeeping or accounting. Is this realistic? When asked why ten years? Lynn responded: "The more experience the applicant has, the more he or she will know—therefore will become productive for us more rapidly." Is there always a direct correlation between years of experience and expertize? Not necessarily. We all know people who have ten years on the job, but only have the equivalent of one year's experience. We also know others who acquire great skill in a very brief period of time.

Recognizing that years alone do not really measure expertize, Lynn rethought her specs. Instead of asking for ten years' experience, she set up a list of factors that the new employee should bring to the job and how strong he or she should be in each of them. By asking the applicants specific questions on each of these factors, she would be able to determine at an interview how much the applicant knew and what he or she had actually done in each area that is important to the job.

Does this mean that years of experience don't count for anything? No. Often the only way a person can gain the skills needed for a job is by actually working in a similar capacity. However, by emphasizing what they have accomplished rather than how long they have done it, we will make a better hiring decision.

Another requirement often found in job specifications is that the experience should have been in "our industry." True, often skills and job knowledge can only be acquired in companies that do similar work, but there are many jobs where the background in other industries is just as valuable and may be even better because the new employee is not tradition-bound and brings creative and innovative concepts to the job.

By limiting the population from which we can choose our new employee to only those in one industry, we may not only eliminate good people, but the job may remain unfilled for a long period of time. The H.R. manager of Associated Health Aids was frustrated. It was six months since the admin assistant to the Marketing Vice-President had left and the position was still vacant. The problem: The VP insisted that his assistant have experience in the health aids field. No applicants with that kind of experience had turned up. When asked why this background was needed, the VP told her that the admin had to know the language of the trade. How long would it take somebody who was not familiar with it to learn that "language?" Probably two to three months. Yet the company had already kept the job open for six months, when in a maximum of 90 days, the lack of this one "critical" requirement could have been overcome.

To avoid falling into the common traps in setting job specification, analyze the jobs carefully. Ask: "What must the applicant have that I either cannot do or do not want to spend time to train them to do?" These should be the essential specifications for that job.

If there are a large number of applicants for a position, we should also determine what preferential factors would be helpful. These factors can be used to help choose from among the applicants who have all of the essential factors. But even in establishing preferential factors, be sure they are realistic and do not eliminate good people. For example, a preferential requirement for a graduate degree when such educational background is not really important for the job may not be wise.

A vital part of every job specification is the indication of the intangible factors—often more significant in hiring the right person than some tangible requirements. Sure, we would all like to hire people with high intelligence, creativity, integrity, loyalty, positive attitudes, enthusiasm and the like. However, when listing the intangibles needed for a job, be sure they are put in proper perspective as it relates to that job. If the job calls for communication skills, specify which communication skills are needed: one-to-one oral communication? ability to talk to groups? telephone communication? writing letters and memos? creating advertising copy or brochures? power-point or other computer based communication techniques?

If the job calls for "attention to detail," specify what type of detail work. If the job calls for working under pressure, indicate what types of pressure: meeting daily deadlines? occasional deadlines? unpleasant working conditions? a tough boss? Analysis and description of the intangibles needed is just as important as analysis and description of education, experience and skills required.

By establishing realistic job specifications and screening our applicants to ascertain that they meet these specifications, we will staff our department with qualified people to form the team we need to meet our goals and objectives.

Screening Candidates

Once the job specifications are established, we must now begin our search for candidates. The people currently working in the organization often know other people who may qualify for the open positions.

Promoting or transferring a current employee to a new position is commendable and should be encouraged. Internal candidates are known factors. The company has seen them in action. They know their strengths and weaknesses, their personality quirks, their work habits, their attendance and punctuality patterns and all the little things that months or years of observation uncover. It also is good for employee morale and motivation. The problem, however, is that it limits the position only to current employees. In this highly competitive world, a company should attempt to find the very best candidate for open positions—and that person may not be currently on the payroll.

There was a time when companies boasted that when the Chairman retired, they hired a junior clerk. Everybody moved up a notch. It is likely that in a large organization there are many highly competent people who are available for filling the new openings and of course, they should be given serious consideration. However, a search for outside candidates may bring to the company skills and expertize that is now lacking and new ideas that often elude people in-bred within the organization.

Charlie used a variety of sources when a vacancy developed in his department and received over thirty résumés. They all looked good. Which ones should he see for the interview? When screening résumés, look for the following:

> *Does applicant meet the basic specifications?*

Don't waste time calling candidates who fail to meet the key requirements for the job.

> *Look for omissions.*

Many résumés omit dates of employment. This may be done to hide periods of unemployment or to leave an impression of having more or better experience than really achieved. One way to overcome this is to have all applicants complete a company application form. This can be mailed to them and returned before we determine who is to be interviewed. If there is a rush to fill the job, telephone or email the applicants in whom we are interested to obtain missing information.

> *Look for inconsistencies.*

An applicant may claim heavy background in one area, yet the companies for whom he or she worked are not involved in that area. For example, Jack's résumé played up his background in marketing consumer packaged goods, but, of his ten year's experience, only two years—several years ago—were with consumer oriented companies.

> *Look for progress.*

For the amount of years in the work force, has the candidate made appropriate progress in terms of advancement and earnings? Compare the backgrounds of the candidates as they relate to the job specifications and then as they relate to each other and select the best for the next stop—the job interview.

*When talking with another person, listen attentively.
Don't assume a bored attitude or allow an "I knew it"
expression to flicker across your features.*

Dale Carnegie

Getting the Most from an Interview

Here are some suggestions on conducting a meaningful interview. After making the applicant feel at ease by a friendly greeting and a few comments on non-controversial aspects of the applicant's background, begin the structured interview with some *open-ended questions*:

"Tell me about your experience with the XYZ Company."

"What background do you have in sales analysis?"

"Describe your most recent project."

On the basis of the responses received, focus on key aspects of the candidate's background in that area and *ask specific questions* based on details of what was done and accomplished.

Mae commented in response to an open-ended question on her most recent project that she had made a market study of the potential of a new product. Specific questions to elaborate and verify what she really did might include:

"How did you obtain the needed data?"

"What problems did you face in getting cooperation from the people involved?"

"How did you solve them?"

"What was the result?"

"Describe the steps you took in your analysis."

"What was the most difficult aspect of the project?"

By asking about specific facets of the project rather than

just accepting her statements, we will obtain a clear view of actual experience rather than the usual generalizations that are so often elicited in a job interview, and it will help identify the real accomplishments of the candidate.

Evaluate Personal Characteristics

We hire not only a person's job skills, but also the personal characteristics that the individual brings to the job. A person with good looks, charm, a gift of gab and a pleasant way makes such a good impression on us that we may be overly influenced by this veneer. To determine the true personality of the applicant, we must look beneath the surface.

By using "situational questions," true personality traits can often be uncovered. A situational question is one in which the candidate is asked to respond on how he/she handled delicate problems in the past or how hypothetical situations might be handled. For example, "A customer calls and is irate. The delivery promised has not arrived and the entire production schedule for this customer is in jeopardy. How did (or would) you handle this?" From the response, we can determine the candidate's integrity (would he/she lie about the delivery?), tact (was the candidate diplomatic?), and attitude (was he/she loyal to the company?).

As the interview is usually the primary tool used in making the hiring decision, it is important that it gives the interviewer the information and impressions needed to make this judgment. Here are ten traps that many interviewers fall into that prevent them from really learning as much as they should know about the people they are considering for employment.

1. *Not structuring the interview*: When Bill returned from an interview with the Chief Accountant of the Goody Gumdrop Candy Co., he was convinced that the interviewer had obtained little or nothing from the interview. Bill reported that the Chief Accountant had jumped from one subject to another—talking for a moment about education, then shifting to some phases of work experience, then back to schooling, over to attitudes, then to job objectives and finally, more questions on work background. Too many interviews are little more than informal chats. In order to make the interview more effective, the interviewer should follow a set pattern that will enable the interviewer to cover all the salient points systematically. It doesn't make any difference whether we start with education, the first job, the last job or objectives, so long as a structure is established and followed to cover all information. However, we must be flexible within the structure, so we don't fail to probe areas of interest just because they may not fit into our interviewing plan.

2. *Interviewing for the wrong job:* Some interviewers do not pay adequate attention to the job specifications. Barbara applied for a job analyst's position. The interviewer asked all kinds of questions on every aspect of H.R. administration except job analysis. Before an interview, study the specifications. Be familiar with the details and implications. Frame questions that will bring out those aspects of the applicant's background that indicates knowledge (or lack of it) of those specifications.

3. *Letting the applicant dominate the interview:* A savvy applicant can so dominate the situation that he or she

only tells us what is most favorable and manages to deemphasize negative facets. The good interviewer must maintain control. When we have an applicant who doesn't let us get one word in, who twists our questions to fit his or her desires, who keeps adding information which is not relevant, but is designed to boost his or her background, *cut it off.* We may say, "That's most interesting, however, would you mind giving me specific details on... (then indicate the specific area)." The best way to counteract an applicant's attempt at domination is to insist that he or she answer our questions to our satisfaction.

4. *Playing God*: One of the major complaints applicants have about interviewers is that they condescend to them. They act so superior that they feel uncomfortable. Because the interviewer has the power to hire or at least to refer the applicant on for further consideration, there is a tendency to "play God" and smugly savor this power. A little humility will pay off in better rapport, and a more effective interview will win friends for us and for our company.

Don't assume an air of importance. Never allow the other person to feel he is inferior to you in any sense.

Dale Carnegie

5. *Signaling the right response*: Some interviewers are so anxious to fill a job, they help the applicant respond correctly to their questions. They signal the expected answer "This job calls for ability to handle people. You do have this ability—don't you?" Nobody ever says, "No."

6. *Stifling the applicant*: When Henry was interviewed, he never had a chance to tell about his qualifications. The

interviewer first told him about the company, then he told him about the job, then about his own work. When he finally did ask a question, he interrupted Henry before he could finish his answer. An interview is a two-way conversation. If only one party dominates it—applicant or interviewer—it will not accomplish its purpose.

Susan stifled her applicant in another way. She wrote down everything the applicant said. It's OK to take occasional notes, but a word-by-word transcription will stifle the interviewee and keep the interviewer from listening fully to what is being said.

7. *Playing the District Attorney*: Martin loved interviewing people. His great joy was to "catch them" in some inconsistency. He would repeat questions in several forms to ascertain that the answers were the same. If he found an "error," he would pounce on the victim. He bragged about all the "phonies" he exposed, but more often than not the inconsistencies were inconsequential and he not only lost good potential employees, but left a poor impression on those applicants he interviewed.

8. *Playing Psychologist:* Just because we took Basic Psychology in college does not qualify us to be a psychologist. Some interviewers assume far more psychological knowledge than they have. They look for hidden meanings in everything the applicant says. They ascribe Freudian motives to work experience, family relations, attitudes and even casual comments made by applicants. The fact that they are not really qualified to make these judgments does not bother them one bit. They are so absorbed in their "psychological evaluations," they fail to determine if the applicant can or cannot do the job.

9. *"Falling in love" with the applicant*: Sometimes an interviewer is so impressed with one aspect of an applicant's presentation that it dominates the evaluation. It may be a person's appearance or charisma, or it might be the possession of a specific skill that is needed by the company. Although that trait may be impressive, there may be other important facts of the applicant's background that negate it. A good interviewer will recognize that this charm or skill is an asset, but it should be put in proper perspective. A well structured interview which allows for a careful evaluation of each factor needed for success in the job, will help overcome this.

10. *Failure to probe for details*: George was asked a series of questions on whether he had experience in several areas of work in his field. He answered each affirmatively, but to his surprise, the interviewer accepted his answer without probing to determine how much depth he had in each area. George could have easily misrepresented his background by outright false information or by exaggerating his knowledge. Good interviewing requires thorough exploration of the candidate's knowledge. Study the job specifications and frame questions based on what is expected in order to meet those specifications.

By careful planning of an interview and being cognizant of the pitfalls and avoiding them, we can make our interviews more meaningful and our hiring decisions more effective.

Don't interrupt the other person when talking. Let that person talk himself out. If you interrupt him you are implying that what he is saying isn't worth listening to.

Dale Carnegie

Verify

Wherever possible, contact the former employers of applicants in whom we have interest to verify that what they have told us is correct. To get meaningful information, try to speak to the applicant's direct supervisor rather than to the Human Resources department. The supervisor has had day-to-day observation of the candidate, where in most companies the only information H.R. has is what's in the files.

More and more companies are reluctant to give information about former employees to others, but it is worth the effort to try. One way to overcome resistance to giving information is to emphasize that we would like to *verify* information rather than ask for information. Before making a call, prepare a series of questions drawn from the applicant's application, résumé and notes from the interview. Be sure to choose significant aspects of the background to use so we can obtain maximum information in a limited amount of time.

Selecting the Best People

We have read a hundred résumés, interviewed dozens of applicants, and have narrowed it down to three or four people, all of whom have excellent experience and background for the job we are seeking to fill. Which one should we hire? This dilemma is faced by managers each time a job opening occurs. We must make this important decision based on the personal characteristics that make one person stand out from all the others. People with "hire appeal" are more likely to impress us than those who lack this intangible trait.

Experience has shown that unless these characteristics are superficial or contrived, they are indicative of success on a job. They are the human factors that enable people to work well with us, their co-workers, and others within or outside the organization with whom they will interrelate.

Appearance

In most contacts with people our immediate reaction is to their appearance. A person whose physical characteristics, dress, and presence are pleasant, neat and attractive, starts off on the right foot in most interpersonal relationships. This does not mean that we should judge the book solely by its cover, or that we should give preference to handsome men and beautiful women. Neatness, a pleasant countenance and good taste in dress and grooming are important. But be careful not to put overemphasis on appearance.

Barbara is an extremely attractive young woman. Over the past five years, she has had four jobs as a sales representative and has failed in all four. The sales managers were so impressed by Barbara's good looks, they assumed she would make an immediate favorable impression on prospects and become a successful salesperson. However, Barbara had little else to offer. She had been so accustomed to getting by on her appearance that she had never had to work very hard.

Do not interpret this to mean that appearance is not a factor to be considered. Many attractive people also have the skill, drive and capability to do a good job. Because many of us tend to put more emphasis than we should on appearance, we should look more deeply into all the aspects of a particularly attractive person's background before making a decision.

We Favor People Like Ourselves

Tom's associates were all alumni of his university. Even though Beth, a native of Iowa, worked in Chicago, three of her staff members were also from Iowa. When Tom and Beth were questioned on why they selected these people, their responses included comments on job qualifications, personality traits and intelligence, but neither manager considered the similarity of backgrounds as being a factor.

One tends to subconsciously favor people whose backgrounds are close to one's own. There is a comfortable feeling when dealing with people who have shared a similar environment or experience. This could be an asset in the sense that working relationships can be developed more rapidly and more easily. However, it may lead to choosing a less qualified candidate. Another limitation when all the people in a work group have analogous backgrounds is the inclination for them to think much alike and therefore, have less exposure to new ideas.

Self-Confidence

When Frank was interviewed he exuded self-confidence. He was not afraid to talk about his failures and unlike people who try to impress interviewers by bragging about their accomplishments, Frank was matter-of-fact about his successes. He projected an image of being totally secure in his feelings about his capabilities. It is likely that Frank will manifest this self-confidence on the job, enabling him to adapt readily to the new situation.

Fluency of Expression

Laura was able to discuss her background easily and fluently. She did not hesitate or grasp for words. When the interviewer probed for details, she was ready with statistics, examples, and specific applications. Not only does this indicate her expertise, but her ability to communicate—an essential ingredient in many jobs.

However, there are some glib people who can talk a great job, but have only cursory experience or knowledge of it. They learn and use the jargon of the field. To determine if an applicant is a talker but not a doer, ask in-depth questions and also probe for specific examples of their work. Glib phonies cannot come up with meaningful answers.

Alertness

Diane sparkled at the interview. She reacted to questions and comments with her facial expressions and gestures. We could see that she was on her toes. Alert, sparkling applicants are usually dynamic and exciting people who give all to their jobs.

Maturity

Maturity cannot be measured by the chronological age of a person. Young people can be very mature and older people may still manifest child-like emotions. Truly mature applicants are not hostile or defensive. They do not interpret questions as barbs by a "prosecutor out to catch them." They do not show self-pity, have excuses for all of their past failures or inadequacies. They can discuss their weaknesses as readily as their strengths.

Sense of Humor

Evan was a sourpuss. At no time during the interview did he smile or relax. Even when we tried to lighten up the interview with a humorous comment, he barely reacted. This may be due to nervousness, but more likely Evan is one of those very serious people who never look at the lighter side of things. They are difficult to supervise and impossible to work within a team. It is easier and much more fun to work with a person who has a sense of humor.

On the other hand, applicants who are too frivolous, who tell inappropriate jokes, laugh raucously or act inconsistently with the situation may be immature.

Intelligence

Although some aspects of intelligence may be measured by tests, we can pick up a great deal about the type of intelligence a person has at an interview. If the job calls for rapid reaction to situations as they develop, (e.g. sales) a person who responds to questions rapidly and sensibly has the kind of intelligence needed for the job. However, if the person is applying for a job where it is important to ponder over a question before coming up with an answer (e.g. research engineer), a slow, but well-thought-out response may be indicative of the type of intelligence required.

Watch for the "Halo Effect"

Rob is a computer wizard. Give him any type of problem that can be solved by a computer and he will develop a program to solve it. His bosses were so impressed with this capability that they promoted Rob to a position which required making decisions that could not be solved by computer. They assumed that because he was so good in one area, he must be good in all areas.

The opposite is the "pitchfork effect." The person involved has one negative characteristic that so dominates our evaluation of that person that we do not see his or her good points.

To avoid the prejudice of halo or pitchfork effects or other narrow approaches of evaluation, we should look at the whole person instead of at disparate traits.

Look for Success Records

"What is past is prologue." In selecting people for a new job, whether it be a promotion from within or hiring from the outside, the most significant factor is their past record. Successful people tend to continue to be successful. People with mediocre records tend to repeat their mediocrity. By evaluating what that person has accomplished in previous jobs or assignments, we can get a graphic picture of what they may do in the new situation. To determine and evaluate success patterns, ask applicants what they consider to be their major contributions in their previous jobs.

When Lee applied for a sales job, he had no specific experience, but his record of success in his previous administrative job showed that he could face and solve complex problems in a variety of areas. The Sales Manager recognized that this was a major asset in selling and selected Lee rather than some of the more experienced salespeople who were competing for the job. Within a few months, Lee proved that his pattern of success carried over into this new position and was on his way to becoming one of the best salespeople on the staff.

The way a person perceives the job also tells much about the candidate. Betty was the office manager of her company. Her major achievement was to keep the work flowing, putting out fires, and assuring that each assignment was completed on time accurately. That is good—if we want a "maintenance" type individual, one who can maintain operations as they are. However, if we need innovation or creativity, it would be better to seek someone who has introduced new systems which improved productivity or had reorganized a department to make it more efficient.

The accomplishments of which the applicant is proud of, also give more insight into his or her thinking about the nature of the work. In answer to the question of achievement, Gary, a candidate for a human resources executive position, proudly described how he created a bowling league and softball tournament for his company. His competitor for the position, Eileen, explained how she introduced a suggestion program which resulted in several cost-saving innovations. On the basis of these responses, which one is the better candidate?

Warmth

This very important intangible asset is a major ingredient of "hire appeal." It is difficult to describe but we know when it is there. The warm person is empathetic and shows real concern about the matters discussed. This person will talk freely about interpersonal relations. He or she is comfortable at the interview and makes us feel comfortable. An individual with this type of personality is at ease in any environment and will most likely fit into the department rapidly and naturally. They are likeable people and easy to live and work with.

Sensitivity to Feedback

The applicant who understands what we are projecting not only in our questions and in our comments, but with our body language will probably do the same on the job. This is an asset which is invaluable in the workplace. People like these are easy to train. They readily accept and implement instruction and criticism and work well with their peers.

Naturalness

A person who is natural and relaxed is probably a well integrated person. However, do not automatically negate a nervous applicant. To reach such a person and determine what latent characteristics may exist beneath his or her uneasiness calls for skill, patience, and determination. Their nervousness may be masking their real selves.

Giving Information to the Applicant

An important part of the interview is giving the applicant information about the company and the job. All the work and expense undertaken to get good employees is lost if the applicants we want don't accept our offer. By giving them a positive picture of the job at the interview, we are more likely to have a higher rate of acceptances.

When and what to tell about the job

Some interviewers start the interview by describing the job duties. Some give the applicant a copy of the job description in advance of the interview. This is a serious error. If an applicant knows too much about a job too soon, he or she is likely to tailor the answers to all of the questions to fit the job.

For example, we tell a prospect that the job calls for selling to department store chains. Even if the applicant has only limited experience in this area, when we ask, "What types of markets did you call on?" guess which one will be emphasized.

The best way to give information about duties and responsibilities is to feed it to the applicant throughout the interview—*after* we have ascertained the background of the applicant in that phase of the work. For example:

Interviewer: What types of markets did you call on?

Applicant: Drug store chains, discount stores, department stores, and mail order houses.

Follow this by asking specific questions about the applicant's experience in each of these markets. If the department store background is satisfactory, the interviewer might then say: "I'm glad you have such a fine background in dealing with department store chains as they represent about 40 percent of our customer list. If you should be hired, you'd be working closely with those chains."

If the background in this area was weak, the interviewer might say: "As a great deal of our business is with department store chains, if you should be hired, we would have to give you added training in this area."

Most interviewers give the applicant an opportunity to ask questions about the job and the company at some point (usually at the end) of the interview. The questions asked can give some insight into the applicant's personality and help us in our evaluation.

Are the questions primarily of a personal nature? (Such as vacations, time off, raises, and similar queries), or are they about the job? People who are only concerned about personal aspects are less likely to be as highly motivated as job-oriented applicants. Their questions can also be clues to their real interest in the job. If we feel from these questions that a promising candidate might not be too enthusiastic about the job, it gives us another chance to sell the prospect on the advantages of joining our company.

We are always 'selling' when we interview. It's important that we present our company and the job in a positive and enthusiastic manner. This doesn't mean that we should exaggerate or mislead the applicant. Tell the applicant any negative factors about the job at the interview, but show how the positive aspects outweigh them. For example, "This job does require you to work overtime for the first few months to acquire our complex technical training, but once you have mastered our system, it will enhance your expertize in this field."

Whether we are considering a current employee for promotion or we are hiring from the outside, it is imperative that every step be taken to assure the right decision is made. Be alert to the dangers of personal likes and dislikes, overemphasis on appearance and the halo or pitchfork effects. Look for a pattern of success in the past, a positive attitude toward the job, the type of intelligence patterns related to the job, and a warm, natural, mature personality.

Sum and Substance

> Before evaluating résumés, set up a list of key requirements. Unless the applicant meets these specifications, there's no point arranging for an interview.
> Don't take a résumé at face value. Read between the lines. Look for hidden negative factors.

- Have all applicants complete a company application. The résumé should be used as a supplement not a substitute for the application.
- Before conducting an interview, review the job specifications as well as the applicant's résumé and application form.
- A good interview should be structured, but flexible enough so that follow-up questions can be asked.
- Put the applicant at ease by asking non-threatening questions at the beginning of the interview.
- Check the references of prospective employees by speaking to his or her direct supervisor, not the H.R. department.
- When comparing candidates consider the whole person, not just work experience. Avoid the halo or pitchfork effects.

5

ENHANCING PERFORMANCE

Phil accepted the congratulations graciously. He had won the club championship for the third consecutive year. A reporter from the local paper asked: "Phil, you're our undisputed golf champ. What advice can you give the rest of us on how we can improve our performance?" Without hesitation, Phil responded: "It begins with the way you tee up."

Preparation

All performance whether it be on the golf course or on the job starts with preparation. Before the first ball is hit or the job assignment is undertaken, it is what is done to prepare for it that will make the difference between adequate and superb performance. In golf, teeing up is not just putting the ball on the tee, but all that has been done before the game to master it.

Technical Competence

The first step is to acquire as much knowledge about the subject as possible. Competency in one's job just as in any sport, starts with learning the basics and then the more complex aspects of the procedure. Becoming technically proficient in the field of one's endeavor is essential for top performance.

Darlene was intrigued by the new technologies in medical diagnosis and treatment. As a nurses' aid at Mercy Hospital, she observed but did not operate this new equipment. At every opportunity, Darlene went down to the department where this equipment was being used. She spoke to the technicians and was given literature she could study. She was particularly interested in the use of the ultrasound machine, which is used to identify many internal problems. She then enrolled in a training program, and became certified as a Registered Diagnostic Medical Sonographer and was transferred to full-time work in this capacity. Most people obtaining this certification would be satisfied to get such a job, but Darlene wanted to be more than just a good worker; she aimed to be the best possible technician. She continued her studies, and volunteered to work on special projects with the physicians using the equipment. In a relatively short time, Darlene was the most technically knowledgeable sonographer in the hospital and was on her way to a successful career in this field.

Training

Training does not stop when one has acquired technical competence. Even the best athletes will continue to train no matter how successful they are. They know that the need for training never ends.

Sam is a successful salesperson who does not believe he will ever complete his training. "There is so much I have to learn," he complains. Every year, Sam takes at least one training course in salesmanship or product knowledge. He reserves time every week to read books and listen to training tapes. This has resulted in Sam's continuing improved performance in servicing his customers and increasing his sales.

Teach Others

Another way to perfect our own skills is to teach others. Not only does this enable us to systematically review what we have been doing and reinforce it for ourselves, but one often learns from the trainee. Questions asked and suggestions made by the trainee can lead to more knowledge about one's own field.

Ann is the supervisor of word processing for a political action committee. With election time nearing, she hired two additional operators and had to train them. In order to assure that these trainees would be taught rapidly and efficiently, Ann set up a training plan. The process of developing this plan forced Ann to rethink many of the techniques that she had been using herself. She recalled some short cuts and special approaches that she had not used in years and came up with some new ideas. Once the training began, the interaction between Ann and the trainees stimulated her to improve her own performance and increase her personal productivity.

Trying

Champions never say. "It can't be done." They try to find a way to overcome the obstacles. Even champions don't always win, but they never lose without first trying to win.

Norman Strauss, an industrial painting contractor in New York City, was confronted with a major problem. His bid for the job of painting Madison Square Garden, New York's largest indoor sports arena was due by the end of the week. The major problem was painting the ceiling, which was 110 feet above the ground floor. The usual way of reaching the ceiling was constructing a pipe platform on which the painters would stand when they sprayed the ceiling. The cost of building the platform was the same for all bidders. The only way to significantly reduce the bid would be to find some way to paint the ceiling without constructing the pipe platform. Everybody knew this couldn't be done, so why bother?

But Norman Strauss did not give up easily. He believed that to achieve success one must never cease trying to solve a problem. On the way home that evening, Norman noticed an electric company repainting a high street light. To reach this light, they were using a "cherry picker," a truck with an elevator on its roof that could be raised to various heights. "Why not use cherry pickers to reach the ceiling at the Garden," Norman thought. Investigation the next day brought out that it was feasible and economical. Strauss was able to submit a significantly lower bid than his competitors and obtained the job.

Think

The final step in preparing for enhanced performance is thinking. Before commencing the game or the job, it is essential that it be thought out. A good golfer thinks out how he or she will play the hole before making that first drive. A superb performer thinks out how the job will be performed before beginning the project.

In a complex operation, as much time must be given to the planning as to the work itself. Before making a sales call, the successful sales representative thinks carefully about all of the possible problems that may develop and how they can be handled. Executives think about every ramification any of their decisions may cause before making that decision. This is also true for top performers in the theater, cinema, television, and in sports.

We can become superb performers by careful preparation for all of our endeavors, becoming technically proficient, and never ceasing training, teaching others, and keep trying—especially when things get tough.

The Performance Process

Performance standards are usually based on the experience of satisfactory workers who have done that type of work over a length of time. Whether the standards cover quantity or quality of the work or other aspects of the work, they should meet these criteria:

Specific: Every person doing a job should know exactly what he or she is expected to do.

Measurable: The company should have a touchstone against which performance can be measured. Measuring performance is easy when a standard is quantifiable; it is more difficult (but not impossible) when it isn't quantifiable. When a numerical measurement isn't feasible, some of the criteria may include timely completion of assignment, introduction of new concepts, or contribution to team activities.

Realistic: Unless standards are attainable, people consider them unfair and resist working towards them.

The Performance Results Description (PRD)

Enhancing performance—our own and that of our associates must be accomplished in a systematic manner. It starts with a look at our own position and the results that we are responsible for at the end of the day, month, and year. It continues both up and down in the organization to ensure there is alignment from the very top to the bottom.

The first step is to determine exactly what we wish to accomplish on this job and how it will be measured. To do this we must design a Performance Results Description (PRD). Unlike the prototypical job description that focuses upon what activities or tasks that should be done, the Performance Results Description is a picture of what the job looks like when it is being done well.

It is a results-oriented view that allows managers and employees to plot a path from the organization's vision, mission, and values to the individual's measurable job objectives. The Performance Results Description not only helps them discover and delineate individual job functions—which we refer to as Key Result Areas (KRA's)—but it correctly measures successful completion of those areas through clearly defined performance standards. This document is an alignment tool that establishes clear-cut individual accountability throughout the team, department, and organization.

As this is done, everyone in the organization is focused on accomplishing the vision, mission, values, and job objectives on a daily basis. This tool helps delineate and measure goals, provide clear-cut responsibilities, and establish accountability. People use technology to monitor a car's speed and performance with the speedometer and gasoline gauge. Leaders help define performance by identifying Key Result Areas and relevant performance standards in the workplace. This system frees people to measure and monitor their own performance while minimizing the need for traditional systems of measurement and discipline.

This view starts at the top with the organization vision, mission, and values, then moves to individual results that are always in alignment with the team, his or her manager and the mission of the organization.

When we maximize the performance process, we create an environment through our leadership where people are free to achieve the results the organization needs to stay competitive and exceed customer expectations; while at the same time assuring employee's personal and professional growth.

Major Components of the PRD

In developing the PRD for a job, we must determine:

> What is the purpose of this job? In other words, why does this job exist?
> What are we committed to in this job and why?
> What are the Key Result Areas—the areas in which specific results must be accomplished that, when achieved, fulfill the job function?
> Are these goals in alignment with the position goal, the vision, and mission of the organization?

Performance Standards Should Be Specific

To assure that these Key Result Areas are determined satisfactorily the performance standards should be specific, measurable, attainable, results-oriented, and time-phased. Among the things to be specified are:

› Deadlines
› Costs
› Duties
› Activities required to accomplish the Key Result Area
› Skills, Knowledge, and Abilities
› What is needed to accomplish this Key Result Area?

Performance Standards Should Be Measurable

Performance standards are tangible, measurable conditions that must exist before the job can be done well. These standards are focused on results, not activities. They should be outcome oriented.

Although we may create our own standards, once written, they are negotiable to the point of agreement with the next level of management. During the performance it can be shown that each standard was, or was not, accomplished. This makes it objective instead of subjective and removes fear from the performance review process.

Here are some "Acid-Test" questions used to determine the strength of a performance standard:

› Is it within our control or domain?
› Are we measuring results or just quantifying activities?
› Where are we expecting perfection?
› Is there any chance of misunderstanding the terms or

language? For example, words such as: "good", "many", "effective", "well done", "successful", "best", etc., are not measurable nor easily agreed on.

Any fool can criticize, condemn, and complain but it takes character and self-control to be understanding and forgiving.

Dale Carnegie

Below is a sample list of performance standards. Of course each job requires individual analysis. These are presented as an example to illustrate the process.

➤ A minimum of 30% of business increase in 2010–2011 fiscal year has been from new customers.

➤ All staff have completed their mandatory yearly recertification within one month of the anniversary of their date of employment, as required in certifying agency standards.

➤ All staff members have attended one training meeting per week in the past six months.

➤ Customer complaints about late deliveries have been reduced by 20% during 2010–2011 fiscal year.

➤ The restructuring of the employee orientation meeting to make it more enjoyable for the staff has been completed by June 15, 2010.

➤ The sales team has increased the level of repeat business from current customers in the pharmaceutical field by 17% between April 1 and September 30, 2010.

➤ The amount of break-ins and vandalism in our branch office has been reduced by 50% during 2010-2011 fiscal year, resulting in 10% lower insurance premiums.

> All graphic designing deadlines have been met every time with each client.

Formal Performance Appraisals

Usually before in most organizations, a formal evaluation of performance is conducted annually. Many leaders add an informal appraisal semi-annually or quarterly as a means of helping associates be aware of their progress.

Importance of Formal Appraisals

> They provide a framework for discussing the person's overall work record. The leader can use this meeting to recognize an employee's past successes and provide suggestions for even greater contributions.
> They enable leaders to measure all members of the group against the same criteria.
> They provide helpful data for determining what type of additional training associates need.
> In many companies, they're the primary factor in determining salary increases and bonuses.
> Their formality causes them to be taken more seriously than informal comments about performance.
> They can be used as a vehicle for goal setting, career planning, and personal growth.

Downside of Performance Appraisals

> They can be stressful for both leaders and staff members.
> It make some leaders so uncomfortable making associates unhappy that they overrate their performance.

- Many formal systems are inadequate, cumbersome, or poorly designed, which creates more problems than solutions.
- In some appraisals, good workers are underrated because their supervisors are afraid that these workers might become competitors.

Choosing the Best System

There are many formal appraisal systems that can be used. Let's look at the most frequently used programs:

Trait-based Systems

The most common evaluation system is the 'trait' format, in which a series of traits are listed and each is measured against a scale from unsatisfactory to excellent. Here is a typical example:

Traits:

- Quantity of work
- Quality of work
- Job knowledge
- Dependability
- Ability to take instruction
- Initiative
- Creativity
- Cooperation

Ratings:

Excellent 5-points; Good 4-points; Average 3-points; Needs Improvement 2-points; Unsatisfactory 1-point—this system seems on the surface to be simple to administer and easy to understand, but it's loaded with problems:

- *A central tendency:* Rather than carefully evaluating each trait, it's much easier to rate a trait as average or close to average (the central rating).
- *The "Halo Effect":* As discussed earlier in this book, some managers are so impressed by one trait that they rate all traits highly. Its opposite is the "pitchfork effect."
- *Personal biases:* Managers are human, and humans have personal biases for and against other people. These biases can influence any type of rating, but the trait system is particularly vulnerable.
- *Latest behavior:* It's easy to remember what employees have done during the past few months, but managers tend to forget what they did in the first part of a rating period.

As the trait-based appraisal is measured in numerical terms, it is tempting to use the scores to compare associates. Some companies encourage the use of the bell curve in making these ratings. The Bell Curve concept is based on the assumption that in a large population most people will fall in the average (middle) category, a smaller number in each of the poorer than average and better than average categories, and a still smaller number in the highest and lowest categories.

The trouble with the use of the bell curve in employee evaluations is that small groups are unlikely to have this type of distribution—and it may work unfairly against top and bottom level workers.

For example, suppose that Carla is a genius who works in a department in which everyone is a genius. However, Carla is the lowest-level genius in the group. In a bell curve for that group, she would be rated as "unsatisfactory." In any other group, she probably would be rated "excellent."

Or suppose that Harold's work is barely satisfactory but that his entire group is performing below average. Compared to the others if we use a bell curve, we have to rate him "excellent."

Every manager and group leader should be carefully informed about the meaning of each category and the definition of each trait.

Understanding *quantity* and *quality* is relatively easy. But what is *dependability*? How are *initiative, creativity*, and other intangibles measured? By developing training programs that include discussions, role-plays, and case-studies, standards can be established that everyone understands and uses.

Establish criteria for ratings. It's easy to identify superior and unsatisfactory employees, but it's tougher to differentiate among people in the middle three categories.

Keep a running log of each employee's performance throughout the year. It isn't necessary to record average performance, but we should note anything special that each person has accomplished or failed to accomplish. Some notes on the positive side may say, for example, "Exceeded quota by 20 percent," "Completed project two days before deadline," or "Made a suggestion that cut by a third the time required for a job."

Notes on the negative side may say, "Had to redo report because of major errors" or "Was reprimanded for extending lunch hour three days this month."

Make an effort to be aware of personal biases and to overcome them.

Gather information. Have specific examples of exceptional and unsatisfactory performance and behavior to back up the evaluation.

Results-based Evaluations

Rather than rating people on the basis of an opinion about their various traits, a more effective appraisal system focuses on the attainment of specific results. Results-based ratings can be used in any situation in which results are measurable. This system is obviously easier to use when quantifiable factors are involved (such as sales volume or production units), but it is also useful in intangible areas such as attaining specific goals in management development, reaching personal goals, and making collaborative efforts.

In a results-based evaluation system, the people who do the evaluation don't have to rely on their judgment of abstract traits, but instead can focus on what was expected from their employees and how close they came to meeting these expectations. The expectations are agreed upon at the beginning of a period and measured at the end of that period. During that time, new goals are developed to be measured at the end of the same period.

Here's how this system works:

> For every job, the manager and the people doing the job agree on the KRAs (Key Results Areas) for that job. Employees must accomplish results in these areas to meet those goals.
> The leader and the people assigned to the job establish the results that are expected from each person in each of the KRAs.
> During a formal review, the results that the associate attained in each of the KRAs are measured against what was expected.

> A numerical scale is used in some organizations to rate employees on how close they came to reaching their goals. In others, no grades are given. Instead, a narrative report is compiled to summarize what has been accomplished and to comment on its significance.

Some companies request that associates submit monthly progress reports compiled in the same format as the annual review. This technique enables both the associate and the leader to monitor progress. By studying the monthly reports, the annual review is more easily compiled and discussed.

When dealing with people, remember you are not dealing with creatures of logic, but creatures of emotion.

Dale Carnegie

The 360° Assessment

Multilevel assessments have become an increasingly popular approach, used to identify how a manager is viewed by his or her bosses, peers, subordinates, and even outsiders (for example vendors and customers). Usually referred to as 360° assessment, such reviews have been adopted by companies like General Electric, ExxonMobil, and other Fortune 500 corporations.

People do not see themselves as others see them. We perceive our actions as rational, our ideas as solid, and our decisions as meaningful. Traditionally, performance is evaluated only by one's own manager. This does give us insight into how our work is perceived by that person, but he or she is not the only person with whom we interact.

Even more complex is the evaluation of senior managers,

who frequently are not evaluated at all. When these executives are assessed by peers and subordinates, they may learn things about their management style that they were not aware of. Many are shocked to find out how people perceive them and, as a result, take steps to change their management styles.

Despite the advantages of multilevel assessments, there are also potential drawbacks. Feedback can hurt. Evaluators may not always be nice or positive. Some people see their role as assessor, as an opportunity to criticize other's behavior on the job.

Another flaw concerns conflicting opinions. Who decides who is right? Or what if an appraisal is biased? If the evaluator does not like the person being evaluated, the responses might be skewed negatively; if the assessee is a friend, the evaluation might be skewed positively. Often, people rating their bosses or other senior executives fear it is dangerous to be completely truthful.

In order to ensure that the 360° assessment has a better chance of producing a change, it is recommended that:

> The appraisal is anonymous and confidential.
> To have sufficient knowledge of the person being rated; the appraisers should have worked with the appraisee for at least six months.
> Appraisers should give written comments as well as numerical ratings. This enables their evaluations to be more specific and meaningful.
> To avoid "survey fatigue," don't use 360° assessments on too many employees at one time.

Employee Evaluation Interviews

Whether a point or results-based system is used, the results must be communicated to the associate. When supervisors are asked what aspect of their job they like least, firing employees is usually first, but right behind it is the evaluation interview. Supervisors do not mind telling good things to their people, but are uncomfortable in discussing shortcomings. Of course, employees feel the same way. They'd dread the evaluation interview and often are nervous, tense or defensive. To make this interview meaningful and productive, both parties should approach the meeting with the positive feeling that this is a constructive exercise.

Preparing for the Interview

Effective appraisal interviews must be carefully planned. Before sitting down with the associate, the leader should study the appraisal itself. It is helpful to make a list of the major areas to be covered. Note all the positive aspects of the performance—not just the areas where improvement is needed. Study previous appraisals. Note all of the improvements that have been made since the last appraisal. Prepare pertinent questions about past actions, steps to be taken for improvement, and future goals.

We should recall all we can about the employee's behavior patterns. Does he or she have any special problems or idiosyncrasies? If this person is known to be belligerent, negative, emotional or in any other factor that may make the interview difficult, be prepared to deal with it.

The meeting should be scheduled a few days in advance. Suggest that the employee review his or her own performance before the meeting. Many companies give the employee a blank evaluation form and ask them to rate themselves. This gives them the chance to give a serious and systematic look at their own performance and prepare them to discuss it at the meeting.

Discuss the Performance

Once rapport has been established with the interviewee, we should point out the areas of the job in which the person has excelled and those in which the standards were met. By giving specific examples, the employee will know that we really are aware of his or her positive qualities. Encourage the employee to comment.

Listen attentively, and then discuss those aspects of performance or behavior which did not meet the standards. Be specific. It is far more effective to give a few examples of where the employee has fallen below expectations than to just say, "Your work is not up to our standard." Performance standards should be clearly spelled out and understood by employees. It should be no surprise to them to be told that they are not meeting those standards. By showing them work with excessive errors, or reminding them of missed deadlines, would be accepted in a more positive way.

In every instance our concentration should be on the work, not on the person. Never say: "You were no good;" say: "The work did not meet the standards."

If the problems are not related to performance, but behavior, give illustrations of this as well—"Over the past several months I have spoken to you about being late. You are a good worker, your opportunities in this company would be much greater if you could only get here on time everyday."

Get Employee's Suggestion for Improvement

Once the situation has been presented, instead of making recommendations for improvement, ask the employee for his or her suggestions. Some employees will resist this. They will present excuses, alibis, and rationales for past actions rather than look forward to future improvement. Listen to them empathetically and encourage them to get it all out of their system. Once this is done, they will be more amenable to face the real situation and come up with viable ideas.

Ask, "In what way can I help you improve your performance?" Accept their recommendations where possible and work out a plan of action on how this can be accomplished. It is often helpful to suggest added training on the job or through outside sources.

We know our people and if in our judgment this employee is unlikely to come up with constructive suggestions, we should be be prepared to propose a few of our own.

Set Goals

If goals had been set at the previous annual review, reevaluate them. If they were met, congratulate the employee and learn just what was done to accomplish this. If they were not met, find out why, and determine what can be done to meet them over the given period of time.

The appraisal interview is not just a review of the past, but a plan for the future. Ask: "What would you like to accomplish over the next twelve months?" Elicit production goals, behavioral changes, and plans for advancement. This could also include personal goals such as obtaining additional education, participation in professional or trade association activities or other off the job endeavors that will enhance his or her career. As the manager, we should be supportive, but not make any promises or give false hope for advancement or career growth that may be beyond what we can offer.

Have the employee write down each goal then next to it indicate what he or she plans to do to achieve the goal. Give one copy to the employee and keep one copy with the employee appraisal form. Next year, use this as a part of the appraisal interview.

Most of the important things in the world have been accomplished by people who have kept on trying when there seemed to be no hope at all.

Dale Carnegie

Summarize

At the end of the meeting, we should ask the appraisee to summarize what has been discussed. Make sure that he or she fully understands the advantages and disadvantages of performance and behavior, the plans and goals for the next period, and any other pertinent matters. Keep a written record of these points.

Unless the employee is doing a poor job and this evaluation is a "last chance" before termination, end the meeting on a positive note—"Overall, you have made good progress this year. I am confident that you will continue to do a good job."

The employee evaluation process, if properly managed, can be a highly stimulating experience for both the employee and the supervisor. The interview should not be a confrontation, but a meaningful two-way interchange that leads to commitment of the employee to reach out for improvement and set and implement goals for the coming year that will lead to a more productive and satisfying work experience.

Performance Appraisals Dos and Don'ts

✓ Do develop a reservoir of goodwill. Be trustworthy.
✓ Do let the appraisee review all the data before the meeting.
✓ Do start with the positive.
✓ Do be a coach.
✓ Do put the spotlight on success.
✓ Do use accurate data for our assessment.
✓ Do coach, and correct. Depersonalize the mistakes.
✓ Do let the other person save face.
✓ Do praise the slightest improvement. Be hearty in our approbation and lavish in our praise.
✓ Do expect improvement.
✓ Do develop a mutual plan of improvement.
✓ Do revise the PRD, and set new performance standards where appropriate.
✓ Do end the appraisal with reassurance and a big reputation to live up to.

Try to adhere to these **don'ts:**

✓ Don't betray confidences.
✓ Don't save up any unpleasant surprises.
✓ Don't nag or whine.
✓ Don't be an adversary.
✓ Don't focus exclusively on failure.
✓ Don't criticize, condemn, or complain.
✓ Don't launch a personal attack.

✓ Don't humiliate the other person.

✓ Don't expect miracles.

✓ Don't ignore him or her until the next appraisal and expect much improvement.

✓ Don't end the appraisal on a negative note.

Sum and Substance

➤ For every job, set performance standards that are clearly understood and accepted by those who will perform the job.

➤ When people know what is expected of them, they can monitor their own performance on an ongoing basis.

➤ If the trait method is used to evaluate staff members, be careful to avoid the dangers of central tendency, the halo and pitchfork effects, personal biases, or an emphasis only on the most recent behavior.

➤ Results-oriented evaluations measure actual performance against predetermined expectations.

➤ Don't fear the performance review. It can be a beneficial and worthwhile experience. We can make it even more valuable by going into the review prepared to handle it in a constructive manner.

6

....

BE A COACH

P robably the most challenging part of the leader's job is
molding the individual team members into a dynamic,
interactive, high-performance unit. We have seen how
athletic coaches shape up their teams and as leaders of our
work teams, we can learn from them.

We do this by helping the members of the team develop
their talents to optimum capacity. We keep our team alert to the
organization's goals and to the latest methods and techniques
that will enable them to reach those goals. We help them learn
what they don't know and to perfect what they do know.

A good example is Bob, an experienced salesman recently
hired by a company. Because of his successful background,
Bob did not expect his manager to give him much training.
He assumed he would be oriented about the product line
and sent into the field. But Bob's manager insisted on giving
him the same extensive training as a less experienced sales

trainee. Bob understood this. He had been a champion runner in high school but his coach at the university had given him as much attention and training as those team members who had never competed before. Successful managers keep this in mind when bringing on a new employee. Even if he or she has had previous experience, it is necessary to work on the company's approaches to the job, which may differ from the employee's past experience. Most managers will not hesitate to do this with a person who has had no previous experience, but often neglect it with experienced personnel.

Helping Team Members Take Charge of Their Jobs

Our work group or team is made up of individuals. Each person in the group contributes to the success of the team's mission. To do that, each member must be skilled in the work he or she performs and motivated to do it superbly.

Here are some suggestions that have worked for many leaders:

> The leader encourages associates to master their jobs. When workers know their work well and perform it in a professional manner, they are on the track toward mastery of their work life. The coach not only trains new members of the group in the basics of their jobs, but works with all the members to keep them on the cutting edge of the latest technology, methods, and innovations. In addition, the leader encourages members to take the initiative in adding to their knowledge, to read, to take courses, to attend seminars, to learn from others—not just about specific aspects of the functions currently performed, but to broaden their knowledge of their profession or skill area. This gives

associates a feeling of comfort and confidence when faced with new challenges that arise.

➤ Training never ceases. Techniques of training can be learned by observing the athletic coach. The professional trainer, whether he or she is a coach or a manager, will start training with a thorough orientation on what must he acquired during the training. This can be done in group sessions (if more than one person is being trained) or by individual discussions. Training aids such as manuals, films, or tapes are helpful during this time.

Elena, the manager of data processing for a housewares distributor has an enviable record of success in getting new people started rapidly. When a new employee joins her department, Elena works with that person almost exclusively for the first few days. She says, "The more time I spend up front, the better the success rate." During this initial training, Elena gives her people thorough preview of the basics of the computers used in her department—no matter how much experience the new employee has already had. She says this gets them started correctly and helps eliminate any bad habit carried over from previous jobs.

➤ Training does not end when the new employee is allowed to work independently. No matter how long a person is on the staff, continual training and retraining should be a part of the manager's job. Successful leaders do not concentrate the training effort only on those people who are not performing satisfactorily, but make a practice of working with all of their people on a regular basis. Just as a coach of an athletic team is constantly on the alert to identify areas where improvements can be made for each team member, successful supervisors seek to work with each of their people to hone their skills, so they can become even more effective in their jobs.

› Managers should have periodic individual training conferences with each of their people alongwith group meetings for all their staff. The manager should always be on the alert for any variations in the performance of each subordinate and give them suggestions and coaching to improve.

Aim for excellence. In most teams there are members whom we know can perform better. They do satisfactory, even good work, but we see in them a potential that is not being reached.

An example: Cathy, team leader of a market development team, felt that one of her associates, Christine, was one of those persons. She set up a meeting with Christine and told her: "Your work is good, I have no complaints about it, but I know that you could and should do better. Had you been less bright, I would've been satisfied with what you've been doing; but I see in you the capacity to be one of the very best people in this company. By being satisfied with mediocre performance, you're not aiming high enough. Let's together develop a plan to help you achieve what you are capable of achieving."

They jointly set goals and plan to reach them. Standards were established so they could measure how close Christine was getting to those goals. They met periodically to evaluate her progress. Within a few months, Christine was doing significantly more effective work and was on her way to an exciting and satisfying career.

› Get the members to participate. As discussed earlier in

this book, it has been shown that when people participate in decisions that affect them, they're more likely to work to achieve them. When a new project is assigned, instead of telling the assignees how to do it, we should work together with them in setting the procedures. Giving them some control over the way it will be done is another way of helping them take charge of their jobs.

> Encourage creativity. Most people feel they have some control over their jobs when their suggestions and ideas are taken seriously. Nobody expects that all of their suggestions will be accepted, but they do expect that they will be given serious consideration. We should create a climate of innovation. This will give associates the opportunity to criticize current practices and come up with their own original ideas. The old adage "If it isn't broken, don't fix it." must be replaced with "If it works now, it's probably obsolete."

Ten Tips on Coaching Associates

1. Meet with each associate on a regular basis to identify what that person can do to become more effective and what we can do to help.
2. Don't wait for a formal performance review to confront poor performance. Take action to correct it as soon as it is observed.
3. Keep a running record of each associate's progress. Include examples of successes and failures. Note areas where improvement is needed. Specify recommendations for that person's growth.

4. In training associates, keep in mind that people master tasks in small steps. Build the training by first giving the associate small tasks, then work up to more complex tasks.

5. Encourage slow learners by praising their efforts and reinforcing the training to help them catch up.

6. Rather than working to achieve several goals at once, help associates build their skills by working on one goal at a time. Once on the way to meeting it, add another goal.

7. We should be a role model to associates by our own pursuit of learning and our application of new approaches to the work.

8. Pass on tips, information, and ideas to team members. This may take the form of articles we read, Internet resources we e-mail to them or sharing new concepts orally.

9. Assign associates responsibility for all or part of a project and give them the leeway to do it without any interference.

10. If the coaching session doesn't result in improvement, ask these questions:

   • What was the purpose of the coaching session?
   • What did I do to achieve the purpose?
   • What action resulted from the session?

Have the team member answer the same questions, and compare the results.

Coaching the Team

Irrespective of work done in teams today, it is not enough to train each member of the team to perform exceptionally. Equally important is bringing together individuals into a coordinated working unit.

For a new team, it starts with a thorough orientation on the objectives of the team—what is expected from each associate, and from the team as a whole. This can be done in group sessions or, when a new member is added—one on one.

Let's look at Erica, leader of an information technology team. When the team is assigned a new project, Erica spends the first day or two of the assignment discussing it with team members—both individually and as a group. She draws on the experience that various team members have had with similar projects and together they plan the entire operation. As the project proceeds, she keeps tabs on each associate's progress and jumps in with assistance, added training, or whatever is needed to make them more effective on the job.

Give Pep Talks

Just as the coach of an athletic team gives pep talks to the team before the game and during breaks, team leaders find that pep talks stimulate production, and reinvigorate members when their enthusiasm wanes. A pep talk is more than yelling 'Go, team. Go!' The effective team leader provides the team with understanding of what they need to change to be more effective team members and works with them to make those changes.

Pep talks help push the team forward for a short term, and often that's enough to pull them out of a rut. For more lasting effect, we must keep the team alert to their progress. It is important to praise every accomplishment, celebrate the success of reaching interim goals, and give recognition to team members who do outstanding work.

Good leaders like good coaches, train people to give pep

talks to themselves. By showing associates that they have confidence in their abilities and in helping them build up self-confidence, managers are performing one of the most important functions of their job as manager/coach. Successful coaches work with people to keep up their spirits when they are depressed, to retrain them when they forget the fundamentals of the job, to revel with them about their triumphs, to understand their personalities, and model motivational programs to take advantage of these factors. Effective coaches do not give up easily when a few people do not meet their expectations. They work with their people and do their best to bring them at par with the high standards set for the team.

Managers can accomplish this by knowing their people and understanding their individual differences. As pointed out earlier, all people are not alike and one of the major errors in attempting to motivate people is to assume everybody wants the same from their jobs. It may be necessary to tailor a special motivational program for each employee. More commonly, supervisors find that each person is motivated by many different things. However, there are certain factors that can be built into most motivational systems.

Good leaders recognize superb performance as well as every improvement. When special achievements are accomplished, the leaders should praise the team and reiterate how the cooperative efforts of the team members contributed to the achievement. One manager makes a practice of having an impromptu pizza or ice-cream party when a significant part of a project is successfully finished; another manager hosts a barbecue at his home for all members and their significant others when a particularly complex project is completed.

Both Coach and Trainee Must Believe in the Vision

One of the most important concepts in coaching is having a vision or end goal in mind. Without that, people often lose sight of the importance of making the required changes. How we create this picture of what is possible is the central component of this step in the coaching process.

People with a clear vision of what the end result of coaching is, tend to move in that direction more quickly than those without. But it is critical the goal be owned by both the coach and the trainee. Without that sense of ownership, motivation may be lost. We focus on motivation and buy-in even more in the next step of the process, but this is where direction and motivation really begin.

Establish the Right Attitude

How well we really know our people may be determined by how quickly we know that we have the right people for the job and how they are motivated. This step is a critical part of the process of effective coaching. Without it we would spend a great deal of our time just overcoming resistance.

We often hear that people resist change. It isn't true, People resist being changed when they:

1) don't see the need,
2) don't want to do it, or
3) believe that the change is not possible for them.

Whenever people are asked to change without their buy-in, they create resistance. The effective coach creates an atmosphere where people are consistently motivated to attain high performance levels.

Provide Resources

The effective manager assures that all the resources needed for the training process are available. These include providing time, money, equipment, training aids, information, and upper level buy-in and support and most importantly, a personal commitment to success by everyone involved.

We must ensure that the appropriate resources are in place and available. Nothing is as frustrating as being promised something and then not getting it. It can make everyone feel like they have been set up to fail.

Identify Strengths and Opportunities for Improvement

Practice also allows the coach to identify strengths and opportunities for improvement. Some of the points to consider here are:

- ➤ How to encourage others to succeed
- ➤ How closely to monitor and when to let go
- ➤ How to hold others accountable for progress
- ➤ How to reinforce. Making progress is one thing, but without a way to reinforce and keep it in place people may quickly go back to the way they did things before. One of the biggest fallacies managers hold to is the assumption that if people know something, they will do it. People don't do what they know; they do what they have always done.

Some of the skills we must look into post reinforcement of coaching are:

- ➤ Empowering people to get results after they have learned new skills

> ‣ Giving the right kind of feedback
> ‣ Following up
> ‣ Handling non-performance issues
> ‣ Handling mistakes and people who get off track

Reward Achievement

One of the best ways to cement growth and progress is to reward it. What we reward gets repeated. What gets repeated becomes habit. Change is uncomfortable. That is why people often revert back to their former ways quickly if reinforcement and rewards are not there. Habit is stronger than knowledge. Suggestions on how to reward and praise has been discussed in Chapter 3.

Be a Mentor—Develop Others to be Mentors

One of the best approaches to develop our people is to encourage experienced associates mentor trainees. For example, a high-ranking manager takes a younger employee under his or her wing and becomes that person's mentor. This gives that person not only a head start for advancement, but will teach him or her know-how about the work, the subtleties and nuances incumbent to the company, and the "tricks of the trade."

It would be a major benefit to organizations if everybody had a mentor. As leaders, we should consider mentoring a job requirement not only for ourselves, but for all experienced team members. By structuring a mentoring program, and assigning the best people on our team the responsibility of mentoring a new associate, we take a giant step forward in making the newcomer productive and on the way to personal growth.

Organization leaders are busy people. Often they just don't have enough time to give to associates, particularly to newcomers in the team. One solution: appoint an experienced team member to mentor the newcomer. Don't always select the same member to be the mentor. Every associate should have the opportunity to undertake this role.

A structured mentoring program requires that people chosen to be mentors be willing to take on the job. Compelling someone to be a mentor is self-defeating. Everybody is not interested in or qualified to be a mentor. However, if in our judgment the person who declines the assignment is really qualified, but is shy or lacks the self-confidence, we should have a heart-to-heart talk about how by accepting the task, both the member and the team will benefit. New mentors should be trained by experienced people in the art of mentoring.

Both the mentor and the person who is being mentored benefits from the process of mentoring. Obviously, those who are mentored learn much more from the process, but equally important is what the mentors gain by sharpening their skills in order to pass them on. It heightens the mentor's sense of responsibility as they guide their mentees through the maze of company policies and politics. It also makes them more effective in their interpersonal relationships.

Ten Tips for New Mentors

When we are assigned to be a mentor, we should learn as much as we can about the art of mentoring. If we have had a personal successful experience with a mentor, use that as a model. If not, seek out another member who has been a successful mentor and learn from him or her.

Here are ten 10 things to keep in mind:

1. *Know the work:* Review the basics. Think back on the problems previously faced and how you dealt with them. Be prepared to answer questions about every aspect of the job.

2. *Know as much as we can about the company:* One of the main functions of a mentor is to help the trainee overcome the hurdles of unfamiliar company policies and practices. More importantly as a person who's been around the organization for some time, know the inner workings of the organization, the true power structure, the company politics.

3. *Get to know the mentee:* To be an effective mentor, you must take the time to learn as much as you can about the person you are mentoring. Learn about his or her education, previous work experience, current job, and more. Learn his or her goals, ambitions, and outside interests. Observe personality traits. Get accustomed to his or her preferred ways of communicating face-to-face, written memos, telephone, e-mail, Twitter, texting, etc.

4. *Learn to teach:* If you have minimal experience in teaching, pick up pointers on teaching methods from the best trainers you know. Read articles and books on training techniques.

5. *Learn to learn:* It is essential that we keep learning not only the latest techniques in our own field, but developments in our industry, in the business community, and in the overall field of management.

6. *Be patient:* Some people learn slower than others. This does not mean they're stupid. If the person you are

mentoring does not catch on right away, be patient. Slow learners often develop into productive team members.

7. *Be tactful:* You are not drill sergeants training a rookie in how to survive in combat. Be kind. Be courteous. Be gentle—but be firm and let the trainee know we expect the best.

8. *Don't be afraid to take risks:* Give the mentee assignments that will challenge his or her capabilities. Let the mentee know failures may occur, but that the best way to grow is to take on tough jobs. Failures should be looked upon as a learning experience.

9. *Celebrate successes:* Let the trainee know you are proud of the accomplishments and progress he or she made. When something especially significant is achieved, make a big fuss.

10. *Encourage our mentee to become a mentor:* The best reward we can get from being a mentor is that once the need for mentoring is done, [the mentee] carries on the process by becoming a mentor.

The successful man will profit from his mistakes and try again in a different way.

Dale Carnegie

Correcting Errors

Even the best people will make errors in their work from time to time. It is the manager's responsibility to correct these errors. To maintain morale and to get the best from our people, we must do this without causing resentment or making the associate feel inadequate or inferior. Although we may become frustrated, upset or even irate about the situation, this is not the time or place to lose our temper, rant and rave and bawl out the person who made the error. Address any situation as soon as it comes up. Unsure of our ability to communicate it well, we often wait until the situation reaches intolerable proportions, and then we explode in a rage. So act early, while the situation and our responses are manageable.

The Nine R's in Correcting Errors

Here are some suggestions on how to diplomatically correct errors, teach the associate how to correct them and avoid making future errors.

1. *Research*
Do the homework to make sure you have all the facts before discussing it with the associate. The aim is not to build a case as much as gather information. You must keep an open mind and look behind the facts to better understand motivations.

2. *Rapport*
When we meet the person who has made a mistake, it is best to begin by putting that person at ease and reducing the anxiety. One way to do this is to begin with honest appreciation that is supported by evidence. Instead of just giving a general compliment, choose a behavior that you have observed. Maintain a policy of keeping the business relationships warm so the other person is open to your input.

Conduct the discussion in private. Don't say or do anything that may cause the person to feel embarrassed or lose face in front of others. Adopt the attitude and actions we want the other person to exhibit. If we speak quietly and calmly, it is likely the other person will do so in return. If we view the fault as small and easy to correct, the other person may adopt the same attitude.

3. *Relate to the Situation*

Essential to success while correcting a problem is to focus on the problem and not the person. Eliminate personal pronouns and depersonalize the problem. It was the action that was wrong, not the person who did it. Give the other person a chance to explain what happened and then let that person know what you know about the problem. Listen to understand and to determine whether he or she is accepting responsibility or blaming and avoiding responsibility. The goal is to gather facts and information to be able to accurately identify the problem and determine why it happened. By reducing defensiveness and not jumping to conclusions, different perspectives will surface, and the root cause of the problem should be identified.

Instead of attaching a negative label or trait to the individual, phrase the comments in non-accusatory terms. Here are some examples:

Instead of saying: "There is not enough information about safety matters in the report," say: "This report is very comprehensive; it might be even more effective if the section on safety were more detailed. . ."

Instead of commenting: "Why were you so careless about these statistics?" If appropriate, supply an appropriate action step. "Joe Smith has the newest numbers you need. Can you get with him today?" or "Will you call Mary Ross at X-Tech to let her know the corrected shipping date?"

How the associate relates to the problem—their actions, attitude, and behavior in this decision—will determine the next moves.

4. *Restore Performance*
The purpose of this step is to remedy the problem, to reduce the chance of the mistake happening again, and to restore the person's performance. It also involves planning to devise a way to keep the problem from occurring again.

This step should be handled differently with the associate who accepts responsibility than with the one who blames and avoids taking responsibility. With the responsible employee, effective questioning, listening, and coaching can be used to encourage him or her to suggest ways to correct the situation. Involve the associate in the problem analysis and decision-making process.

For the "blaming" or "avoiding" employee, the manager may first need to reaffirm performance expectations and coach them to accept responsibility and to restore accountability.

5. *Reassure*
This step is focused on the person. Obviously a person who has made a mistake may feel, to some degree, like a failure and is likely to be less inclined to approach the next opportunity with confidence. Therefore, the manager needs to help the associate see the situation in a different context.

The associate needs to be reassured of his or her value and importance to the organization and of the manger's support and encouragement. The associate should leave the meeting motivated to achieve optimal performance because he or she perceives a solid relationship with the organization.

The "blaming" or "avoiding" person should leave with a sense of accountability and an understanding of what the company's expectations are. That person should also understand that we are interested in and committed to his or her success and growth.

6. *Retain*
If we handled the previous steps well, we have increased our chances of retaining the person, and enhanced his or her commitment. It also reinforces the morale of our whole team. This builds trust and increases the level of commitment and work ethic.

7. *Restate*
However, sometimes people resist the efforts to repair the situation, or refuse to relate to the issue. In such cases the next move is to restate the facts, the seriousness, the policy and the proper remedy to the issue. This gives the person one more chance to do the right thing.

8. *Reprimand*
When people refuse to accept responsibility, we may have to formally remind them in some way prior to further action. Most organizations have established policies and procedures that must be followed before disciplinary action can be taken. This is particularly important in companies with contracts either with individual employees or with a labor union. How to conduct such reprimands will be discussed in chapter 9.

9. *Remove*
Sometimes we find that the employee is not a good fit for a particular task, project, or in some cases a major part of the

department's activities. We may need to explore what his or her strengths, interests, and goals are and search for a better fit within the company. It is an injustice to employees and companies when we perpetuate a situation where individuals feel that they can never succeed.

The last resort after attempts to coach them for desired performance have been unsuccessful is to remove them from this area of responsibility—to replace, reassign or release them from the organization.

Remember to comply with all the organizations policies when making this decision.

Sum and Substance

> The leader's job is to ensure that all members of the group or team know the organization's goals and the latest methods and techniques that will enable them to reach those goals. They help them learn what they don't know and to perfect what they do know.

> Just as a coach of an athletic team is constantly on the alert to identify areas where improvement can be made for each team member, successful supervisors seek to work with each of their people to hone their skills so they can become even more effective in their jobs.

> To avoid resentment and assure cooperation when correcting an associate's mistakes, focus on the problem, not the person.

> In dealing with associates who have failed to meet performance standards, follow the 'Nine Rs' approach.

7

DELEGATING WITHOUT FEAR

Delegation is the process of assigning by the manager to one or more of his or her associates, the duties or responsibilities to be performed as well as giving the authority to commensurate with those responsibilities. By establishing and communicating performance standards, the manager creates accountability on the part of the delegatee. It is through the sharing of responsibilities by means of assigning combined with the assignment of authority and accountability that managers manage.

Reasons for Delegating

Managers may choose to delegate for many reasons. Some of these are:

> By shifting some of their workload, it frees them to work on other tasks that may be more complex, of higher priority, or require personal attention.

> Delegation is an opportunity to develop people via stretch assignments.
> It allows them to take advantage of the specialized skills or preferences of others on the staff.
> Delegation enables to distribute the workload, thus speeding up the process of getting things done.

Don't Be Afraid to Delegate

In order for most supervisors or managers to accomplish all their activities, it is essential that they delegate some of their work to their subordinates. Yet many managers are afraid to delegate. Let's look at some of these reasons:

> Fear of change and the unknown
> Inability or unwillingness to let go or known tendency to micromanage
> Believing that they are the only ones who can do the job properly
> Unwillingness to give up doing something they enjoy
> Lack of faith in subordinates' ability to perform and believing that "if we want something done right, we have to do it ourselves"
> Belief that it's quicker and easier to do a task personally than to train others to do it
> Ego-related fear that subordinates will outperform them or that they will become dispensable
> Lack of confidence in one's own ability to train, manage, and lead others
> Fear of imposing on or making demands others; not wanting to be "the bad guy"
> Fear of conflict

Building Self-Confidence

Most of the fears listed above are due to lack of self-confidence. One example is Paul, who fears that if a subordinate does too good a job, he or she will be a threat to him. "If the boss sees that one of my people can do what I can do, my job may be in jeopardy."

Although there have been situations where a manager has been replaced by a lower salaried subordinate, it usually has not been primarily due to this reason. As a matter of fact, the opposite is more usual. Most companies consider how effectively managers build up the capabilities of their people by evaluating their management skills.

By becoming as proficient as he can in his job, Paul will earn the respect of his supervisors and because he knows he is good at his work, it will build up his self-confidence. By making his people more effective in their work, he will be able to accomplish more in those aspects of the job that are of greater importance than those he has delegated to his subordinates.

Ellen's fear is more common: "If my subordinate messes up the assignment, I will be the one held responsible." All managers are held accountable for the work of their subordinates. In order to be assured that the work she has delegated to others is done correctly and on schedule, she should follow these steps in planning the delegation:

> Determine the capabilities of each of the people in the work that is to be performed. To delegate an assignment to one who is not able to do it properly dooms it to failure. If we do not have anybody who is capable, we have no choice but to

do it ourselves. If this is the case, the highest priority should be to train somebody to be able to handle this, so that the next time there is a need to delegate, a capable person will be available for the assignment.

➤ Determine how much training, guidance, and supervision the delegatee(s) might need in terms of time and attention, as well as what other resources might be necessary.

➤ Determine how delegating to this individual or these individuals will impact their current workload.

➤ If the delegatee does not report directly to us 100% of the time (e.g., with project teams), determine how to handle any potential conflict in priorities or issues with their other supervisors.

➤ In addition to keeping an eye on the task at hand, we should keep in mind the human aspect of managing and leading people. We should use interpersonal understanding techniques to see how delegates are feeling about how things are going. We should always be aware of their developmental progress, build their confidence, inspire them to perform and coach them to help maximize their potential. We must create a win-win situations whereby everyone will benefit from the fruits of their labor.

There is only one way. . . to get anybody to do anything. And that is by making the other person want to do it.

Dale Carnegie

Planning the Assignment

For any activity to succeed it must be planned. Too often supervisors do not take the time to prepare assignments.

They know what has to be done and assume by ordering an associate to do it, it will be done properly. Planning starts with having a clear concept of what must be accomplished. Even if one has done this type of work many times, it is important to think it through once again. We must put ourselves in the place of the associate. If we had never seen this project before, what would we want to know? List the objectives we wish to attain, the information needed to attain it, the materials, tools, support sources and whatever else is needed to do the work.

A very important part of the planning is to determine who will be given the assignment. In selecting this person bear in mind the importance of the assignment. If it is one in which it is essential that it be done rapidly and with little supervision, choose a person who has demonstrated ability in the past in this type of work. However, if it is an area where there is adequate time for you to provide guidance, it may be advantageous to assign it to a less skilled person and use this project as a means of training and developing that person's skills.

What is Delegated Should Be Communicated Effectively

Barbara was frustrated. She had given Carol a detailed description of what she wanted to be done and Carol had assured her she understood. Now, a week later, Carol turned in work that was all wrong. Her excuse: "I thought that's what you wanted."

Like many supervisors, when Carol said she understood, Barbara assumed that she really did understand. To be sure that a subordinate understands an assignment, don't ask "Do you understand?" That's a meaningless inquiry. Often the subordinate may think that he or she understands an assigned task, but really doesn't—and in good faith tells us that it is understood. Some people may be embarrassed to tell us that they do not understand and say that they do and then try to figure it out for themselves. Instead of asking "Do you understand?" ask: "what are you going to do?" If the answer indicates that it is not clearly understood, we can correct their perception of the assignment immediately.

Morton was upset. His boss had just given him a deadline that he felt was totally unrealistic. "He's out of line," Morton thought, "There's no way I can do this much work in such a short time. I'll do what I can, but I know I'm not going to make it."

With that attitude, it's unlikely that Morton will meet the deadline. In order to get full cooperation from a subordinate, it is important for that person to fully accept what it is we want. To gain acceptance, first let the subordinate know the importance of the assignment, then get him or her to participate in the planning process. "Mort, this assignment must be in the boss's hands by 10 tomorrow morning. When do you think you can have it?" Morton can now see the urgency of the work and together work out with us a realistic time table, which may include the need for additional help or authorization for overtime work.

Effective delegators design the communication strategy efficiently, thereby effectively presenting the assignment to their delegatees. This includes preparing to address any potential resistance, anticipating questions and concerns, etc.

Give the Delegatee the Tools to Get the Job Done

In Martha's company, computer time is always at a premium. When she delegated a project to one of her people, she neglected to arrange for computer time. As a result the entire project bogged down. Martha had the responsibility to assure that her subordinate had everything needed to do the job. By failing to do so, she doomed the project to failure.

Another type of "tool" the subordinate should be given is the authority needed to accomplish the mission. Martin was instructed to meet a tight deadline on the project. To do this it was necessary to work overtime, but Martin was not given the authority to order overtime work. This delayed completion of the project and resulted in missing the deadline.

Get a Plan of Action

On assignments that will take any significant amount of time, ask the associate to prepare a plan of action before starting the job. This should include just what is to be done, when it is scheduled to be done and what support may be needed.

Paul Cullen, founder of Cullen Electronics was retiring after 30 years on the job. His successor, Frank Ames, decided to have a gala celebration of his accomplishments and appointed his H.R. manager, Mark Lovett to arrange the affair.

Mark was to arrange travel plans for key employees, customers and vendors from all over the country to come to the celebration. Before starting the assignment, he wrote a plan of action to cover every aspect of the assignment including hiring a caterer, choosing the location, arranging for decorations, sending invitations and making airline and hotel reservations for out of town guests. The plan included time tables for starting and completing each phase and indication of what assistance would be needed for each phase. Mark reviewed this with Mr. Ames to assure all was in accord with his concepts. Mark wrote out the plan of action so that everyone involved in implementing the program were able to check at any time how the plan was proceeding and help to catch the problems early.

Set Control Points

Even if one delegates responsibility to the delegatee, managers are still held accountable. To assure that the assignments be performed correctly and on time, control points are set at places where one can check the progress of the assignments and if anything has gone wrong, it can be corrected before it goes too far. Control points are not surprise inspections. The associate knows when they will occur and what is expected at that point. For example, we give Ted an assignment on Monday that must be completed by Friday. We tell Ted: "We will meet tomorrow at 4 p.m. to discuss the project. By that time you should have completed Parts A and B." If at that time we uncover errors, they can be corrected before Ted continues. Another advantage of control points is that if Ted realizes at 11 a.m. that he will not be able to complete Part B by the 4 p.m. control point, he can ask for help early enough to keep the project from falling behind schedule.

Follow-Up

As managers are responsible for the actions of their subordinates, a system of follow-up is an essential management tool. To accomplish this without micromanaging can be a delicate matter.

When managers are constantly looking over the shoulders of their people, it engenders a feeling of distrust—and that can destroy the collaborative, cooperative atmosphere essential to true success.

Follow-up should be done in a particular manner. Instead of constantly overseeing the work or surprising subordinates with unexpected check-ups, the follow-ups should be built into the plan of action. Rather than superimpose a follow-up plan, the manager and the subordinates should develop the plan together. Control points should be incorporated throughout the project. When various phases of the project have been completed, the manager and the people performing the project will need to go over what has been done. The workers should be encouraged to critique the work and perhaps suggest new or additional matters that might be incorporated in the assignment. Of course, the manager would contribute appropriate comments and suggestions as well.

In this way the follow-up becomes part of the participative approach and acts as a stimulus for the subordinate to achieve even greater success in meeting the challenge of the assignment.

People rarely succeed unless they have fun in what they are doing.

Dale Carnegie

When We Delegate, We Do Not Abdicate

Managers should be available to help their people if need arises. When Duncan assigned a new project to Andrea, he told her: "I'm here to help you. If you have any problems, don't hesitate to bring them to me." Andrea took this literally and instead of trying to deal with her problems, she brought them to Duncan. This not only took an inordinate amount of Duncan's time, but did not help develop Andrea's skills.

The next time Duncan delegated a project to one of his people he again noted his availability to help them, but added: "Bring me your problems, but bring with them a suggested solution." This encouraged them to think about the situation and come to their own conclusions. Duncan would rather have them ask him: "Do you think this will work?" rather than "What should I do?"

Upon Completion of the Assignment

There is no one right way to do something. It's all about successfully achieving the desired result in the end. So even if something is not done exactly as we would have done it (most likely it won't be), that's perfectly okay.

Ask ourselves how we performed as the delegating manager. What things did we do right and wrong during this process? What, if anything, would we have done differently? What will we do differently in the future?

Analyze how the delegatee performed? Did he or she rise to the occasion? Was he or she stretched by the challenge or overwhelmed beyond his or her capabilities? Did we get personal feedback on how he or she thought things went? Did we take advantage of this developmental opportunity to provide the delegatee with praise or recognition, with rewards, if deserved, as well as providing fair, open, and honest constructive criticism?

Consider the ways in which your relationship with the delegatee may have changed from this experience and where things would go from here; how one might build on this progress or remedy any damage.

Finally, don't forget that you are ultimately responsible and accountable for the outcome when it comes time to report back to the superiors. As the manager and leader, your duty is to share the credit and celebrate the success with your delegatees. But the flip side of "wearing the crown" is that should things fail, the blame will lie solely on our head. In the end, that is what management and leadership is all about.

By following a systematic approach in delegating, you will accomplish more because other people would be doing those things which are more suited for subordinates freeing you for more significant work. You would also be accomplishing one of the most important roles of a manager—building up the capabilities of your staff. Delegation is one of the best means of giving people the experience important to their own development.

Delegating to Teams

When an organization is structured into teams, work should be delegated and assigned as a team activity. When people have some control over the assignments they get, they approach their work with enthusiasm and commitment.

When the boss gives a complex project, one should present it in its entirety to the team. Discuss with the team how to break the assignment into phases. Delegating each of the phases to individual team members will follow easily. Most members will choose to handle the areas in which they have the most expertise. If two members want the same area, let them iron it out with each other. But if it gets sticky, step in and resolve the problem diplomatically: "Gustav did the research on our last project, so let's give Liz a chance to handle it this time."

Certain phases of the assignment are bound to be tough or unpleasant. No one's really going to volunteer to do them. Have the team set up an equitable system for assigning this type of work.

As team leader, be sure that every member of the team is aware of everyone else's responsibilities as well as their own. In this way, everyone knows what everyone else is doing and what kind of support he or she can give or receive from others.

To keep everyone informed, create a chart listing each phase of the assignment, the person handling it, deadlines, and other pertinent information. Post the chart in the office for easy referral.

Sum and Substance

Some key points concerning delegation:

> Once the objectives have been established, the means of achieving them must be determined, after which the work to be performed and the associated responsibilities must be determined.

> It is because the necessary responsibilities are either too complex, diverse, or voluminous for one individual to handle that the need for delegation arises.

> While delegating work and the associated responsibilities to someone else, one must also delegate the appropriate degree of authority necessary to perform the delegated tasks. Delegation without empowerment will only lead to frustration and failure.

- Responsibility is the obligation of the delegatee to perform the required tasks. Accountability is the obligation of the delegatee to produce the desired results. Ultimate responsibility and accountability is the overarching obligation of the delegating manager to successfully achieve organizational objectives.
- Delegation takes time—planning, communicating, monitoring, etc.—but will save time in the long run. Delegation is not intended to be a quick fix (though it can be sometimes) but a long-term strategic approach to getting things done.
- Important: Remember that delegating responsibility, authority, is not delegating ultimate accountability! The delegating manager is still ultimately responsible and accountable for achieving the end result. Managers and leaders must take the good with the bad.
- Finally, remember the saying: "Delegation is not abdication." And, when successfully completed, it is important not to forget the recognition and the celebration!

8

....

ENCOURAGING INNOVATION AND CREATIVITY

"More, better, faster with less" seems to be the mantra we hear so often today. How do we keep up with the changes and get in a proactive mode to deal with change?

It isn't just change that is so challenging. It is the speed of change. It comes faster each time. It is essential to the future of an organization.

The ability to create new products or systems innovation and develop existing products, services, or systems have been studied in many different ways over the years. Some researchers have sought to uncover and understand what makes a person creative. Others have examined the kind of environment that stimulates creative effort and enables it to thrive. Still others have focused on the development of creative products and services.

For centuries, people have been fascinated by the creative process—the series of ordered steps through which a person or group of people utilize the principles of creative thinking to analyze a problem or opportunity in a systematic, unbiased, and seemingly unconventional way. In recent times, modern research in the social and behavioral sciences demystifies the concept by showing how even modest powers of reasoning, analysis, and experimentation help us attain insights into the nature of innovation and its many faces and expressions.

This increased awareness and understanding captures the imagination of quality-conscious managers worldwide who recognize the enormous benefits of developing the creative powers and problem-solving abilities of their associates. In fact, surveys show that the ability to think creatively—to analyze problems and opportunities in new, innovative ways—is thought to be one of the most valuable skills we can develop within ourselves and within the organization.

Why? Because creative ideas result in new discoveries, better ways of doing things, reduced costs, and improved performances—issues vitally important to business people operating in modern competitive environments.

The Thinking Mechanism

The thinking mechanism of the human brain can be described as consisting of two elements: one part for uninhibited creative thinking and the other for analytical or judicial thinking.

The term "Green-Light Thinking" applies to the thought process most conducive to the generation of ideas. In this aspect, the quantity—not the quality—of ideas is emphasized.

The judicial part of the mind analyzes and evaluates ideas emanating from the creative, uninhibited part. Here, the focus is on the quality of ideas. The term "Red-Light Thinking" is often used to describe this process. "Green-Light" and "Red-Light Thinking" are two different processes and both are good and useful. They just cannot be applied at the same time. We often turn on the red-light when somebody presents an idea because we are thinking judicially before we have a clear concept of its ramifications.

This is not only true of our encouraging innovative ideas from others, but we internalize this and loath to open our own minds because most of our educational processes and systems have been devoted to developing the judicial thinking function (i.e., an ability to make decisions, compare and evaluate situations, distinguish between correct and incorrect, etc.), most people do not realize the extent of their own creative ability. In fact, our potential in this area is always present and can be developed to a much greater extent rather easily. We must never lose confidence in our own creative capabilities.

Keep your mind open to change all the time. Welcome it. Court it. It is only by examining and reexamining your opinions and ideas that you can progress.

Dale Carnegie

Everybody is Creative

Everybody is creative. Unfortunately, the creative juices which flow so easily when nurtured are cut off in most people—from childhood on—by the imposition of over-analysis and conformity by the authoritative figures in their lives. Too often creativity is blocked by red-light thinking:

"Stop this,"

"It's against company policy,"

"We never did it that way."

Instead of looking for reasons not to try new ideas, we should look at new ideas with open minds. Turn on the green light, Explore it further, Expand our thinking about it beyond the obvious.

Gary pondered about an idea that could increase productivity by a simple change in methods. Should he tell his boss? The last time he had made a suggestion, his supervisor rebuffed it. He said it wouldn't work. Never gave him a chance to explain it. Why bother now?

Just because we may believe our ideas may be rejected should not stop us from being creative. It is easy to give in to discouragement, but unless we keep coming up with ideas, we will stifle our own creative capabilities. Innovation must be honed by constant use. People tend to censor themselves by worrying about how others will receive their ideas. Self-censorship is far worse than criticism of others because it makes one feel inadequate. We will make mistakes; we will make suggestions that do not work; we may even be ridiculed by our bosses or our peers. Don't let this stop you. Einstein, Edison, Whitney and Watt were all ridiculed many times. Keep those creative ideas coming.

Blocking Creativity

Every idea is not necessarily going to work or is even worthwhile to pursue. However, by at least thinking about it and talking to others about it, we can explore its viability. If it is rejected, learn the reasons. Do not lose heart. Often the idea, as good as it appears, may not fit the specific application or be appropriate at that time. This does not mean it is not good. It also should not be interpreted as a personal affront. It was the idea that was rejected—not you.

Developing Creativity

Most people do not really believe that they are creative. All their lives they have been taught that creativity is some sort of special talent possessed only by artists, inventors and geniuses—not true. Psychologists have proven that creative thinking can be developed.

Here are some of the things we can do to make us more creative:

Observe

One doesn't have to dream up new ideas to be creative. By observing things around us and applying what we learn from other situations is just as creative as total innovation.

Stan, the manager of Hooper Steel in Las Vegas, noted that as more and more gas stations became "self-service" and no longer had facilities for oil change and lubrication of cars, rapid lubrication stations sprang up to meet this need. Stan used one of them for his car and was pleased with the speed and quality of the work.

For years Hooper Steel had sent its trucks to the service department of the dealer for their regular lubrications. This required sending two people to bring the truck to the dealer (one to drive the other back to the shop in his or her car), leave the truck at the dealer all day, and return later to pick up the truck—again using the time of two people.

"Why not use the rapid lube station for our trucks?"

thought Stan. The result: By sending one driver to the rapid lube station and having that person wait about 30 minutes while the truck was being serviced, Stan saved his company about $1600 a month in out-of-pocket service costs and lost time. In addition they had the use of the truck for most of the day.

Modify

Can we modify an existing product or concept to create something different? The founders of "Think Big" modified standard products by making enlarged versions of them. Their giant facsimiles of popular products ranging from pencils and telephone message pads to animals and furniture created a whole new market in advertising, decoration and novelties.

The growth of computer and electronic industry is based on modification by miniaturizing of electronic systems and components into microchips.

Substitute

Darlene, office manager of Mass Mailers, was having a difficult time retaining personnel in an extremely dull routine job: stuffing brochures and samples into envelopes. The nature of the job was such that it could not be done by the standard automated equipment. Not only was the cost of this turnover expensive, but she could never be sure that somebody would be there to do the job. She reasoned that if so-called "normal" people found this job so boring, perhaps mentally-challenged people might not. By filling the jobs with these "slow-learners," Darlene was able to hire workers who were not bored by the work and have become steady and valued employees.

Eliminate

Gil was irate. His company added still another form for salespeople to complete. How could he be out there selling when there was so much paper work that had to be done? When he complained to his sales manager, she shrugged her shoulders and said they needed the information "upstairs." Gil took all the forms he was required to complete, set them side by side and analyzed what information was required. It became apparent that there was a good deal of duplication of data. Instead of griping about it, Gil designed a new form that would provide the necessary facts to management and was easy to complete. This not only made the salesperson's job easier, but saved the company considerable time and money. An added benefit: it started the company on a systematic review and revision of all forms leading to elimination of many outdated and unnecessary reports.

These are only a few ways the creative juices can be stimulated. By stretching our imagination, by expanding our horizons, by breaking with conventional approaches to problems, we can become more inventive, solve difficult problems and initiate and implement exciting new concepts. This will not only be of benefit to the company, but will give us that great feeling of accomplishment when we see our ideas successfully implemented.

> *The person who goes farthest is generally the one who is willing to do and dare. The sure-thing boat never gets far from shore.*
>
> Dale Carnegie

Group Creativity

Most people visualize the creative person as one working along and generating ideas or inventions like Bill Gates or Steve Job. Actually many creative concepts come from groups of people working together. The interaction and cross-fertilization of ideas stimulates ideation.

The old adage, "two heads are better than one" and it's amplification that many heads are better than a few has been shown over and over again to be true. Group efforts in committees and conferences have helped solve many problems.

One approach that has been used effectively is *brainstorming*. Brainstorming is a technique for obtaining as many ideas on a subject as possible. The difference between the usual kind of meeting and brainstorming is that the objective is simply to generate ideas green-light thinking. To get the most out of a brainstorming session, red-light thinking is banned. Participants may not criticize, analyze, reject or accept any suggestion from any participant no matter how ridiculous or valueless or terrific it may appear to be.

The psychological principle behind brainstorming is called triggering. Any idea can trigger another idea in the minds of a listener. A dumb idea from one person can lead to a good idea from another. By allowing the participants to think freely and not concern themselves with how the idea will be received, brainstorming frees people to stretch their minds, and pave the way for an idea that may have value.

In a typical brainstorming session the group tackles a single subject, announced in advance of the meeting. Once the chair introduces the subject, he or she steps back and becomes just another member of the group. One person is appointed to list the ideas on a flipchart. Ideas are called out and recorded. No comments pro or con are made. Freewheeling is encouraged; the wilder the idea, the better. Success is measured by the number of ideas that are generated. Participants are encouraged to hitch-hike onto ideas that are presented. After the session a committee reviews the idea, investigates, and analyzes them. Only then red-light thinking begins.

Brainstorming is not appropriate for all types of problems, but can be very helpful in many situations. It works best in solving specific problems rather than determining long-term goals or general policies. Some examples of successful brainstorming are naming of a new product, opening new channels of distribution, making jobs less boring and developing non-traditional approaches to marketing a product or service.

Be Open to All Ideas

"Our company is different." How often have we heard this phrase? Many companies feel that they are unique and unless an idea, a process, or a program is created by them, it will not fit their needs. Of course, each company has its own culture and its own individuality, but we can learn a lot from other companies—even those whose business is considerably different from ours.

Get Out of the Rut

When people work together for a long time, they tend to think alike. Ideas presented by one may be accepted by all without critical analysis as all members of the group look at things in the same way. Alfred Sloan, one of the founders of

General Motors, recognized this. The company was about to undertake a major project. All members of the group involved, including Sloan felt it was a good idea. However, Sloan was uneasy about this. He told his group that they should give it more thought, check what problems other companies may have had with similar projects. He tabled the proposal for several months. When they met again about the same many problems that had been overlooked were discussed and what would have been instituted uncritically a few months earlier was *sent* back for serious reconsideration and refinement.

Benchmarking

One of the basic principles of the Total Quality Management concept is that successful companies are not afraid to seek out ideas from other organizations that may help them meet their goals. Indeed, one of the requirements in the Malcolm Baldrige awards—the U.S. government's highest recognition for high-quality businesses—is that participants share the methods and techniques used to achieve the award with all interested parties. This is called "benchmarking."

Direct Competitors

One may ask why a successful company would want to share what made them successful with their competitors. It is true that many organizations will not share trade secrets, but much of what leads to high quality is not so much a "secret" but a process that benefits all.

José operates a small appliance repair business in Gainesville, Florida. He is not doing as well as he feels he could do. José would like to ask Carlos, one of his successful competitors for advice, but knows he will probably be laughed at. Why should Carlos help a person who may take business away from him? But José is not limited to people who are his direct competitors. He learns from a trade publication that a small firm in Pell City, Alabama has overcome many of the problems he is facing. These people are not competitors and are much more likely to share some of their ideas with José. A telephone call or better, a visit to this firm would accomplish this.

Look to Other Industries

Our industry is not unique. Other businesses quite different from ours may have faced similar problems we have and solved them. They may be willing to help us.

One of the shuttle services that transported people from suburban New York to and fro the airports was plagued with complaints. Customers who telephoned for pick-ups had to wait through nine or ten rings before the phones were answered and then were put on hold for another few minutes. Finally, when they reached a clerk, they had to answer a variety of questions about their pick-up even if they had used the service over and over again.

The owner sought help from other transporters in various cities, but all had the same problem and had not solved them. As in most locations, they were the least expensive means of transportation, they felt that their low prices justified the delay.

One of the employees of this company told his boss: "I used to have the same problem when I ordered merchandise from L.L. Bean, a well-known outdoors clothing and equipment mail order firm. I would wait to be served, and then asked my address, credit card, sizes, etc. each time. Now when I call, they have all this on the computer. They answer the phone promptly and once I give them my name and phone number, all they need to know is what I want to order. I'm off the phone in a few minutes."

The owner made an appointment to speak with an L.L. Bean executive, who was happy to give him information about the computer program they were using. Within a few months they had installed a similar program which alleviated most of the problems they were facing.

A few years later he read about an improved system and upgraded his program so that when the caller-ID identified the caller, the computer automatically opened that customer's file displaying all the necessary information instantly.

Encourage Employees to Create Benchmarks

Learning from other companies is not limited to executives. Individuals should be encouraged to increase their skills by seeking out other people in their areas of expertize.

Melissa, a market research analyst, made a practice of attending meetings of the local chapter of the American Marketing Association. At one meeting she sat at the table with Angela, who was currently working on a marketing project that involved the use of some new techniques with which Melissa was not familiar. Angela invited her to visit her office to look over the system. Melissa suggested to her boss that she be allowed to spend some time at Angela's facility to study what they were doing. This resulted in Melissa's learning a new approach to her work which enabled her to do a more effective job for her company.

There is a certain special satisfaction in solving problems on one's own and this should not be discouraged. However, we are not the only ones in the world who have faced these problems. By researching what has been done by others and by seeking help from successful companies and people, much time and effort can be saved and solutions found that will keep us and our company on the cutting edge in our field.

Take a Chance

When Alex was a boy in Chicago, he and his friends were ardent Cubs fans. They were elated when their team won and unhappy when they lost. Alex felt the losses more than his friends. When the Cubs lost, he would be deeply grieved. After a particularly bad season, Alex thought, "It isn't worth it. I'm never going to get so involved with a team that I can feel this bad." From that time on he refused to commit himself to the Cubs or any team in any sport.

Alex carried this concept into all aspects of his life. His philosophy was: "If I don't become too involved, I can never be hurt." In his school and in his jobs, he always took the middle course. Indeed, Alex never did get hurt, but neither did he ever have any real joys. By not taking the chance that someone or something that he supports might not work out, he avoided the "agony of defeat," but never experienced "the thrill of victory."

Don't Fear Commitment

Teresa was all excited. After much thought, she came up with an idea that she felt would solve a major problem she faced on her job. When she presented it to her boss, he scoffed,

"It'll never work. Go back and rethink it." Some people may accept such a rejection, but Teresa was so sure it would work, she continued to refine the idea and in time convinced her boss that it was feasible.

Inventors and innovators have always faced ridicule. Jonas Salk was told over and over again that he was on the wrong track in his pursuit of a polio vaccine. Edison had tried and failed hundreds of times before succeeding in inventing the light bulb. Successful inventors must be willing and able to overcome the doubts and disappointments of defeat after defeat before reaching their goals.

Don't Be Reluctant to Disagree

Most people are uncomfortable when they are in the minority in opposing the way others in their group want to approach a problem. They feel that by disagreeing, the others might look down on them. The safe course is to go along and keep the disagreement to themselves. But if we are sure that the group may have overlooked an important aspect of the problem, it is crucial to risk being rejected and make an effort to present and prove what we believe.

Taking risks does not mean one must be a daredevil. Reasonable people take reasonable risks, but by definition, a risk may not succeed. Successful business executives take risks with every decision they make. However, they maximize their chances of success with careful research and analysis before making a decision. But when that decision finally has to be made, the manager must be willing to risk the possible loss of money, time, energy and emotion. Without risk, there is no possibility of gain.

Champions Take Risks

It is the end of the ninth inning. The Blue Jays lead the Yankees 2 to 1. The first two hitters strike out. Dave Winfield, the Yankee's ace hitter is at bat. The ball comes straight across the plate. Wham! a clean hit. Winfield races to first. He makes it easily. Should he try for a double? In microseconds, Dave must decide if he should play it safe or take the risk of trying for that extra base which would put him in a scoring position. If he fails, the game is over, but by taking a chance he increases the possibility of turning defeat into victory. Winfield is a risk taker and if there's a slightly better chance of success, he'll try for the double. Champions in life as well as in sports will take chances. That is what makes them champions.

What is the Worst that Can Happen?

In his book, *How to Stop Worrying and Start Living*, Dale Carnegie advises that when facing trouble: Ask yourself, "What is the worst that can possibly happen? then prepare to accept the worst; try to improve on the worst."

For example, Gil had not been able to obtain an appointment with Allen, the purchasing manager of a prospective customer. He had phoned, written letters and even "sat on his doorstep"— all to no avail. His colleagues advised him to forget Allen and to use his energies and time to develop other leads. But Gil was stubborn. There must be some way to get Allen's attention. He learned that Allen was to be a speaker at an industry workshop. "If I attend the workshop," thought Gil, "I can approach him after his talk, ask him some questions and then identify myself, so he'll at least know who I am."

His sales managers and co-workers discouraged this. "He'll be so mad he never will speak to anybody from this company again."

Gil responded by applying Carnegie's principles. "What is the worst that could happen? He won't do business with us. That's not so bad because he isn't doing business with us now, so we have nothing to lose."

By taking a chance, Gil reached an "unreachable" prospect and opened a very profitable account for his company.

Develop success from failure. Discouragement and failure are two of the surest steppingstones to success. Study them and make capital of them. Look backward. Can't you see where your failures have helped you?

Dale Carnegie

Being Creative Requires Us to Risk Failure

All of us have failed in various things we tried throughout our lives, but we learn from our mistakes and use what we learn to overcome them. The first time we try something new, it is likely we will not succeed.

When little Tricia tried to put together her first jigsaw puzzle, she cried in frustration. The parts simply wouldn't fit together. But with patience and some guidance from her mother, she began to identify patterns and in a short time her failures turned into successes.

Even when we have experience and know-how, we cannot always be successful. There will be times when we do fail, but we must not let the concept of failure overwhelm us. We should learn from our mistakes and apply what we have learned to overcome our failures.

We must all take risks if we want to make progress in our jobs and in our lives. By careful analysis we can minimize the chances of failure, but we can never eliminate them. Without pain there is no gain. By always playing it safe, we may avoid that pain, but we will never feel the great joy and satisfaction that results from overcoming obstacles and reaching our goals.

Sum and Substance

> The ability to think creatively—to analyze problems and opportunities in new, innovative ways—is thought to be one of the most valuable skills we can develop within ourselves and within the organization.
> In seeking solutions first use "green-light" thinking to develop new concepts, ideas or approaches. Then turn on the "red-light" to analyze and evaluate.
> Some of the things we can do to make us more creative are:
>> Observe and apply what we learn from one situation to solve a different problem.
>> Modify an existing product or concept to fit new situations.
>> Substitute different method for less effective traditional approaches.
>> Evaluate systems and procedures and eliminate duplications or redundancies.
> Use brainstorming to get a plethora of ideas, through group participation.

- > By "benchmarking" we can learn how other organizations have dealt with similar problems as ours.
- > Don't be afraid to take reasonable risks in tackling tough situations.

9

DEALING WITH LEADERSHIP
PROBLEMS

When we are promoted or assigned to a leadership position, we do not automatically acquire the skills and techniques that make us good leaders. We have to acquire them. It starts with earning the respect of our associates.

Be Good at What You Do

People respect professionalism. This does not mean that you have to be able to do the jobs that each of your people do better than them. Indeed, the higher one gets in management, the less likely that he or she can do many of the jobs that are done by their staff. The president of a company is unlikely to be able to operate every type of equipment or computers used in the organization. Even in the lower echelons of management, you would probably be required to supervise people who perform jobs quite different from your own. But, if you do whatever it is that you do in a professional manner, your people will respect you.

Treat People Fairly

Unless you deal with your people with an even hand, you will not only fail to gain respect, but will exacerbate resentment. This does not mean that everybody has to be managed in the same way. People differ one from the other and good leaders learn these differences and tailor the manner in which they deal with each of them and their individualities.

Stick Up For Your People

If your department is having a dispute with another department, you should stick up for your people even if it is not always politically expedient. Carey had tried her best to compete the work needed for a project her colleague, Stan, was working on. Due to technical problems with the new computer software, her people were not able to meet the deadline. Stan roared into her office. "What are your people trying to do? My staff can't start our phase of the project until you get them all the data. And don't give me that lame excuse that the computer is down."

Carey did not want to antagonize her colleague but she knew that her people had been doing their best to get the data and that they were really having those computer problems.

She responded: "Stan, we are just as anxious as you to get the data together, but the computer trouble is real, not just an excuse. I have had the tech people here to fix the problem and it should be on line today."

Give People Credit for What They've Done

Praise accomplishments. Let people know that their work is appreciated. On the other hand, one of the most devastating things a supervisor can do is to take credit for something one of his or her people has done and claim it as one's own.

Listen to Your Associates

Unless one listens, you cannot maintain an ongoing relationship with others. However, listening is more than just standing or sitting with our ears open. We must be active listeners. Active listeners ask questions about what has just been said. They paraphrase: 'So the way I see it is. . ..' When people realize that we really listen to them they know that we respect them and this will lead to more respect for us.

Support Your Staff

As discussed in chapter 6, give them the tools and teach them the techniques that will enable them to succeed in their jobs. Take time—even if it requires you to work extra hours or put off another project—to coach people when needed, to counsel them when they have problems, and to assure them that they are an integral part of your team.

Leadership Blunders to Avoid

Being a supervisor is never easy and it's particularly tough the first time one is promoted to a management position.

Let's look at a few of the common blunders supervisors often make.

Starting Out on The Wrong Foot

The first steps we take when starting our new assignments will set the climate of the department for months to come. If we have been promoted from the ranks, there is a good chance that other persons in the department had also vied for the job. For us to succeed, it's essential that we obtain their cooperation. To minimize their discontent, it is best that we not be the one to announce our promotion. It should be done by the person who made the decision, the boss. He or she should sit down with the unsuccessful candidates and say something like this:

> Tom, as you know you were one of the three people I was considering for the promotion. You were all highly qualified, but as there was only one opening I had to make a choice. It was a tough decision. I chose Susan for the job. This is not a negative reflection on your work, but as Susan has considerable knowledge of the new equipment, I felt that she could make the department more productive sooner. We are growing and additional opportunities will be coming up and you certainly will be considered for them. I would appreciate your giving Susan all the help you can to make this department as good as we know it can be.

When Susan starts, she should not call a meeting and say "I'm the new boss of this department and from now on we're going to do things my way." That is not the way to win friends and influence employees. Instead of calling a meeting, speak to each of the people in the department individually. Share some of your ideas. Elicit some of theirs. Ask for their cooperation. "I can't do this job alone. It is a team effort. I need your help."

As a new supervisor we may be desirous of making immediate and radical changes in the way things are done in the department. Don't! Change should be made by evolution, not revolution.

Dealing with employee-friends

How friendly should a supervisor be with their subordinates? Being too friendly can often interfere with the necessary control we should have, while being too aloof might cause resentment and lack of cooperation. Finding the middle ground is not easy.

Before Barbara was promoted to supervisor of the data entry section, she was particularly friendly with three of the ten women she now supervises. She is now their boss. Should she continue this relationship? She liked these women and didn't want to lose their friendship. However, the other workers in the department were jealous and although Barbara did her best to avoid any indications of favoritism, her actions were frequently interpreted negatively.

Upset about this, Barbara asked the advice of an experienced manager. "Probably some of the saddest things I had to do in my career," he said, "were to break the personal ties I had with former colleagues as I moved up the ladder, but it had to be done. Don't do it suddenly. Phase it out. Gradually cut out the after work socializing and the lunches. Start eating with other supervisors. In the beginning this may hurt your old friends, and you will not be happy, but unless you do this, you will not be able to run your department efficiently and your chances of getting ahead in this company will be reduced."

Lack of Recognition and Use of People's Talents

Claudia and Dave were very creative people. They had many good ideas that could have made the work in their department much easier for everybody. Yet their supervisor, Carla, insisted that everything be done "the way we always did it."

When Carla was chastised by her boss for the low level of production in her department, she fumed: "It's not my fault. My people just don't care about the work." Had she utilized the talents of Claudia, Dave and some of her other associates, not only would their contributions have improved production, but her people would "care about" the work, resulting in even better results.

Dealing with Negativism

In most organizations we will find negative thinkers. They always find some reason to oppose new ideas and argue with others on every point. Let's look at some of the problems negative people cause:

> *Resistance to change:* Even people with a positive attitude are reluctant to change. It's comfortable to keep doing things the way they've always been done. Positive people can be persuaded to change by presenting logical arguments. Negative people resist change just for the sake of resisting. No argument ever helps. They may even sabotage a situation so that they can say: "I told you so."

> *Impact on team morale:* Just as one rotten apple can spoil a whole barrel, one negative person can destroy the entire team's morale.

Control Emotions

It is easy to become impatient with negative people. However, it is not necessary—even if possible—not to show displeasure when somebody is constantly defying us. Instead of thinking "She's up to her old tricks. I'm not going to let her push me around," we must learn to think "She's manifesting her anti-authority feelings. It has nothing to do with the problem or with me." By not taking it as a personal affront, we can deal with it in a logical not an emotional manner.

Set Clearly Understood Guidelines

In dealing with negative people, instead of giving very specific instructions, where ever possible have the associates participate in how an assignment should be performed within deadlines of the work. Give them unambiguous performance standards that must be met, but let them determine what to do to meet them. This minimizes fighting over details and minor matters. Negative people will still find things to object to, but by giving them more control over their work, we eliminate the need to fight them on every point.

Listen to What They Don't Say

Negative people would not hesitate to tell us what is on their minds. However, the real issues may remain unsaid. A diatribe about some perceived mistreatment may be a subterfuge for hiding a fear that we do not like him or her. Often negativism is a cry for help. By filtering out from their complaints the areas that are not mentioned, we may uncover the real reason for the negative attitude.

In responding to such situations, determine what we can say or do at this moment to respond to the real situation as well as the perceived grievance. A non-opinionated, non-judgmental response will encourage the associate to reveal more layers of emotion until he or she feels understood. Once this happens, the person is more likely to cooperate.

If we sense that the employee is afraid that we do not like him or her, after we have approached the immediate problem, make a comment about some of the good things this person has done and reassure the employee of your appreciation and respect.

Work to Build a Positive Relationship

Negative people need constant reassurance. By making an overt effort to build a strong positive relationship with them, we may not change their personality, but we can make an impact on behavior.

Talk to them. Learn as much as you can about their interests, their goals, their real lives. Find out what they want out of this job that they are not getting now. If possible, offer training, support and coaching to help them overcome problems and reach their goals.

It isn't necessary to become their friend, but it is important that we are not their enemy. Take the time to explain your decisions. Ask for their ideas and input. Chat with them informally about non-business matters so they look upon you as a total human being, not just a boss or a representative.

By taking the time to learn about negative people and to change our thinking about them from that of a problematic employee to a human being with problems, we will find a smoother and more productive relationship developing.

Administer Discipline

One of the most unpleasant tasks of managers is staff discipline. When we hear the word "discipline," what is the first synonym that pops into our head? Most people say "punishment." We have always looked upon discipline as a means of punishing employees for violating company rules or not meeting production standards.

The traditional discipline system starts with a reprimand and if that doesn't work, more serious punishments ranging from formal written reports, probation, suspension and finally, termination. It is based on the concept that the employee must pay for his or her crime. This attitude is counter-productive. Punishment is viewed with resentment and hostility. A new approach, affirmative discipline, has been tried successfully by many organizations. This is accomplished through a series of reaffirmations of commitment rather than use of punishment.

Here's how it works:

> *Communication*: The employee is made fully aware of the company's rules and policies during the orientation process. He or she is asked to accept and commit to this policy.
> *Reinforcement*: After the first few months on the job, the employee meets with his or her supervisor and the rules and policies are explained again and the employee renews his or her commitment.
> *Violations*: If a violation of a rule occurs, the supervisor will initiate a conference with the employee and review that person's agreement to be committed to the company policies. The employee is asked to assure the supervisor that

both the rule and the nature of that person's obligation is understood. This is confirmed in a memo signed by both employee and supervisor.

> *Second violation*: If the employee reneges on the commitment and repeats the violation, a second conference is held and the commitment is reinforced.

> *Final conference*: If the employee violates a minor rule for the third time within a specified period or a major rule for the first time, the supervisor asks the employee if he or she really wants to continue being employed with the company. If the employee states that he or she does want to continue, the employee signs a document stating that he or she is aware of the violation and that he or she will commit to abide by the commitment from now on.

> *Termination*: If the commitment is not kept, the employment will be terminated. Companies using this approach report that it is an effective way of maintaining high standards of conduct and employee morale.

Sum and Substance

Qualities of Outstanding Managers

Although individual strengths and abilities may vary, research indicates that outstanding managers view the world in similar ways. The following represent the most commonly observed qualities in outstanding managers and leaders:

> They hold strong values and high ethical standards.
> They lead by example, acting with integrity in both their professional and personal lives.
> They are knowledgeable about both corporate and departmental goals.

- They develop a vision of the future, and are proactive and self-motivated to achieve results.
- They are strong communicators and exceptional listeners.
- They earn trust, credibility, and respect.
- They are flexible under pressure and keep their emotions in check.
- They have a right versus wrong attitude. They invite constructive dissent and disagreement and are open to change and new ideas.
- They simplify ideas, concepts, and processes.
- They nurture the concept of team and respect diversity.
- They take the time to get to know what drives individual team members and enjoy motivating and helping them to succeed.
- They recognize and maximize strengths in others.
- They hold themselves and others accountable for results.
- They are efficient and manage their time effectively.
- They are creative and innovative.
- They exhibit excellent judgment while solving problems, making decisions, and resolving conflicts.
- They are committed to continuous learning and improvement.
- They look at discipline as learning rather than a punishing process.

Ten common mistakes managers make:

1. Relying on their title to gain respect.
2. Contradicting themselves or breaking their word.
3. Taking work-related issues personally.
4. Treating all employees the same versus understanding the diverse qualities and motivating factors of individuals.

5. Setting goals without fully understanding corporate objectives and strategies.
6. Neglecting to plan and prioritize goals of their departments.
7. Failing to clearly communicate objectives and to gain consensus.
8. Continue to do tasks that should be delegated.
9. Fail to act decisively when associates fail to meet standards.
10. Forget to show appreciation and recognition.

Appendix A

....

ABOUT DALE CARNEGIE

Dale Carnegie was a pioneer in what is now referred to as the human potential movement.

His teachings and writings have helped people all over the world become self-confident, personable, and influential individuals.

In 1912, Carnegie offered his first course in public speaking at a YMCA in New York City. As in most public speaking courses given at that time, Carnegie started the class with a theoretical lecture, but quickly noticed that the class members looked bored and restless. Something had to be done.

Dale stopped his lecture and calmly pointed to a man in the back row and asked him to get up and give an impromptu talk about his background. When the student finished, he asked another student to speak about himself, and so on until everybody in the class had given a brief talk. With the encouragement of their classmates and guidance from Carnegie, each of them overcame their fright and gave satisfactory talks. "Without knowing what I was doing," Carnegie later reported, "I stumbled on the best method of conquering fear."

His course became so popular that he was asked to give it in other cities. As the years went by, he kept improving the content of the course. He learned that the students were most interested in increasing their self-confidence, improving their interpersonal relations, becoming successful in their careers and overcoming fear and worry. This resulted in the emphasis of the course being shifted from public speaking to dealing with these matters. The talks became the means to an end rather than the end itself. In addition to what he learned from his students, Carnegie engaged in extensive research on the approach to life of successful men and women. He incorporated this into his classes. This led to the writing of his most famous book, *How To Win Friends and Influence People*.

This book became an instant bestseller and since its publication in 1936 (and its revised edition in 1981), over 20 million copies have been sold. It has been translated into 36 languages. In 2002, *How to Win Friends and Influence People* was named the #1 Business Book of the 20th Century. In 2008, *Fortune Magazine* listed it as one of the seven books every leader should have in his or her bookcase. His book, *How To Stop Worrying and Start Living*, written in 1948 sold millions of copies, has also been translated into 27 languages.

Dale Carnegie died on November 1, 1955. An obituary in a Washington newspaper summed up his contribution to society:

> *Dale Carnegie solved none of the profound mysteries of the universe. But, perhaps, more than anyone of his generation, he helped human beings learn how to get along together— which seems sometimes to be the greatest need of all.*

About Dale Carnegie & Associates, Inc.: Founded in 1912, Dale Carnegie Training has evolved from one man's belief in the power of self-improvement to a performance-based training company with offices worldwide. It focuses on giving people in business the opportunity to sharpen their skills and improve their performance in order to build positive, steady, and profitable results.

Dale Carnegie's original body of knowledge has been constantly updated, expanded and refined through nearly a century's worth of real-life business experiences. The 160 Dale Carnegie Franchisees around the world use their training and consulting services with companies of all sizes in all business segments to increase knowledge and performance. The result of this collective, global experience is an expanding reservoir of business acumen that our clients rely on to drive business results.

Headquartered in Hauppauge, New York, Dale Carnegie Training is represented in all 50 of the United States and over 75 countries. More than 2,700 instructors present Dale Carnegie Training programs in more than 25 languages. Dale Carnegie Training is dedicated to serving the business community worldwide. In fact, approximately 7 million people have completed Dale Carnegie Training.

Dale Carnegie Training emphasizes practical principles and processes by designing programs that offer people the knowledge, skills and practices they need to add value to the business. Connecting proven solutions with real-world challenges, Dale Carnegie Training is recognized internationally as the leader in bringing out the best in people.

Among the graduates of these programs are CEOs of major corporations, owners and managers of businesses of every size and every commercial and industrial activity, legislative and executive leaders of governments and countless individuals whose lives have been enriched by the experience.

In an ongoing global survey on customer satisfaction, 99 percent of Dale Carnegie Training graduates express satisfaction with the training they receive.

About the Editor

This book was compiled and edited by Dr. Arthur R. Pell, who was a consultant to Dale Carnegie & Associates for 22 years and was chosen by the company to edit and update Dale Carnegie's *How to Win Friends and Influence People.* He also authored *Enrich Your Life, the Dale Carnegie Way* and wrote and edited *The Human Side,* a monthly Dale Carnegie feature that was published in 150 trade and professional magazines.

He is the author of more than 50 books as well as hundreds of articles on management, human relations and self-improvement. In addition to his own writings, Dr. Pell has edited and updated such classics in the human potential field as Napoleon Hill's *Think and Grow Rich,* Joseph Murphy's *The Power of Your Subconscious Mind,* James Allen's *As A Man Thinketh,* Yoritomo Tashi's *Common Sense* and works of Orison Swett Marden, Julia Seton and Wallace D. Wattles.

Appendix B

....

DALE CARNEGIE'S PRINCIPLES

Become a Friendlier Person

1. Don't criticize, condemn or complain.
2. Give honest, sincere appreciation.
3. Arouse in the other person an eager want.
4. Become genuinely interested in other people.
5. Smile.
6. Remember that a person's name is to that person the sweetest sound in any language.
7. Be a good listener. Encourage others to talk about themselves.
8. Talk in terms of the other person's interests.
9. Make the other person feel important—and do it sincerely.
10. To get the best of an argument—avoid it.
11. Show respect for the other person's opinion. Never tell a person he or she is wrong.
12. If you are wrong, admit it quickly, emphatically.

13. Begin in a friendly way.
14. Get the other person to say "yes" immediately.
15. Let the other person do a great deal of the talking.
16. Let the other person feel the idea is his or hers.
17. Try honestly to see things from the other person's point of view.
18. Be sympathetic with the other person's ideas and desires.
19. Appeal to the nobler motives.
20. Dramatize your ideas.
21. Throw down a challenge.
22. Begin with praise and honest appreciation.
23. Call attention to people's mistakes indirectly.
24. Talk about your own mistakes before criticizing the other person.
25. Ask questions instead of giving direct orders.
26. Let the other person save face.
27. Praise the slightest improvement and praise every improvement. Be "hearty in your approbation and lavish in your praise."
28. Give the other person a fine reputation to live up to.
29. Use encouragement. Make the fault seem easy to correct.
30. Make the other person happy about doing the thing you suggest.

Fundamental Principles for Overcoming Worry

1. Live in "day—tight compartments."
2. How to face trouble:
   Ask yourself, "What is the worst that can possibly happen?"
3. Prepare to accept the worst.
4. Try to improve on the worst.

5. Remind yourself of the exorbitant price you can pay for worry in terms of your health.

Basic Techniques in Analyzing Worry

1. Get all the facts.
2. Weigh all the facts—then come to a decision.
3. Once a decision is reached, act!
4. Write out and answer the following questions:
   - What is the problem?
   - What are the causes of the problem?
   - What are the possible solutions?
   - What is the best possible solution?
31. Break the worry habit before it breaks you
32. Keep busy.
33. Don't fuss about trifles.
34. Use the law of averages to outlaw your worries.
35. Cooperate with the inevitable.
36. Decide just how much anxiety a thing may be worth and refuse to give it more.
37. Don't worry about the past.
38. Cultivate a mental attitude that will bring you peace and happiness
39. Fill your mind with thoughts of peace, courage, health and hope.
40. Never try to get even with your enemies.
41. Expect ingratitude.
42. Count your blessings—not your troubles.
43. Do not imitate others.
44. Try to profit from your losses.
45. Create happiness for others.

www.ingramcontent.com/pod-product-compliance
Lightning Source LLC
Chambersburg PA
CBHW021928190326
41519CB00009B/945